I0615888

The Webs We Weave

By

The Women of Kent County Correctional Facility

The Webs We Weave

ISBN: 978-0-578-88699-2

Table of Contents

Dedication

This book is dedicated to the women of Kent County Correctional Facility. This would not have been realistic if you women never poured your true emotions into writing with a pen and piece of paper. This book is a book because beautiful women like you opened up and expressed your true heartache and believed in the healing of this book, you all gave meaning to this book.

In my stay it could have been a living hell for me because of not knowing the culture, people, or just simply not following the rules. You all made my stay as beautiful as you could within our circumstances. We all helped each other overcome a lot of emotions involving the heartache of being away from the ones we truly love. This is for all the women that stayed strong and held each other up. We did it!!! And y'all can't forget 1,2,3,4 on our way up out the door!!!!

Foreword

Ivory white cement cinderblocks. That's all we see. The color of the bunks, the walls, the ceiling, the fixtures, blue mattresses, grey pinstriped blankets, and a splash of white for the sheets. These colors become our enemies. I was so frightened, confused, dazed, angry, and also timid. I had no idea of the hurt that encamped this place.

"Oooh you gotta be quicker than that!" An inmate stated as she grabbed up the book she just won.

"Damn, why she in here?" The girl with the purple and red weave said to herself. This young girl I noticed that kept on staring whispered, "I wonder what she did?"

An elderly woman with missing teeth loudly chimed in on the conversation. "I think I seen her from somewhere before."

This woman, who initially I believed to be a man, was certain she recognized the woman. She stared into my eyes and said, "Yeah, she do look familiar! No. No, real talk I know her from somewhere."

Yes, the first day that I was actually deemed an inmate. Conversations were just conversations, and what you were on the outside was the only piece of you that people truly saw.

"Elaboration please!"

"Girl I'm in here because I pled very early in my case. Didn't you see it all over the news and Facebook? The shit was embarrassing. I hate trolls that be extra." I told my newfound Bunkie, a girl named Nikki. She was a few years older than me but had her share of bids. This was her 36th time in jail. That was scary for me because it was my first time incarcerated.

"Girl tell me what happened; you don't even seem like the type of person to be in jail in the first place." I was thinking the same thing as I went back in time to tell a story of hurt and utter ignorance.

April 21st, 2017 was Shelly's birthday, who was Reign's, my Goddaughter, best friend. Reign asked if my boyfriend and I would get a room for the event. We ended up booking a room; well actually, he did. He planned everything out with them before I left for work that day.

Later when I got home, my oldest son and newborn baby weren't in the house. I had no idea where they could have been, especially since it was 11:00pm. Normally when you get off of work, the first people you want to see are your children. That truly bothered me that they weren't anywhere in the house. I decided to go out and find them. I showered and got dressed. The only thing on my mind was finding my kids. I called my kids' dad, and I was sent to voicemail. This made me worry even more. Next, I called the hotel room directly. Finally, he answered the phone. His was slurring words and his tongue sounded loose. That angered me so much. It wasn't anything new, but this time he had my children out of our home.

Inmate Nikki asked, "Girl what was he drinking?" I responded, "Seagram's Gin or what he drunk a fifth of."

She laughed and said, "damn I would have been mad, so where was your kids at then?"

"Okay let me finish. I'm about to get to that." So my boyfriend answers the phone and asks me, 'how the hell are you calling this room woman, you got a G.P.S tracker on me?' All disorderly and belligerent. Rather than getting upset, I tell myself that I will deal with him when I see him. I then tell him to put Reign on the phone.

"God mom you coming? I got the kids with me; you know they good," Reign said.

"Oh ok, I'm on my way now."

Thirty-two minutes later, I am in room 107. The sight was of pure disgust. His voice over the phone did not do justice to what I saw in person. He had thrown up all over his body. The friend he was with was standing on the bed damn near declaring himself king. To who? To hell if I know. There was yelling, laughter, all sorts of trash on the floor, words written in red lipstick on the mirror. Our three-month old was in a diaper, just a diaper being held by a stranger. He was screaming and this stranger was standing there looking confused and stoned. The air conditioner buzzed high above the TV. My oldest son sat right next to a bottle of alcohol, looking upset. There were teenagers running in and out in bathing suits laughing and giggling. I had enough. My mind was in a trance. I quickly get on the phone and call my brother to come and get the kids and also my drunk boyfriend and his friend. I try and tell him that my brother is about to come and get the truck. That didn't sit well with him at all.

"You not driving my truck nowhere" he yelled.

"Why the fuck are you drunk when you supposed to make sure they straight? Why did you bring my kids out of the house???! What the fuck is wrong with you? Damn my baby is here and you're not even coherent. You can't even focus your eyes!! You are fucking despicable, ignorant ass bastard!"

"Fuck you I'm gone" he screamed as my brother grabbed him and the baby's car seat.

"Give me my damn keys," he threw them to me as he stumbled out of the hotel room with the baby diaper bag across his chest.

"God mom, can we keep the kids for a few more minutes before y'all leave?

"Why?"

"Shelly need to go to the ATM to give money to the room for breakfast in the morning."

"Naw, they going with my brother."

Keys in hand, my god daughter, the birthday girl and I walked to the parking lot trying to find the truck he drove in. We found the truck, jumped in and my favorite singer was in the deck: Bruno Mars. Low and behold my favorite song was on. 'Jump in the Cadillac ....' As we sang the chorus together, blasted at volume 50, we turned into the nearest gas station so that Shelly could get her money from the ATM. I was feeling high off of Bruno Mars and the replaying of my favorite tune at least a ½ dozen times, so I felt calm. I was okay.

"What time is it y'all?" I yelled because he music was so loud.

"1:07am," Reign yelled back.

"Ok I want to go to the liquor store because by the time I make it home the stores gonna be closed. I guess we can go to the one around the corner. "

As we pull up to the drive thru liquor/corner store I ask for my favorite drink. A pint of Captain Morgan Long Island Tea.

"Yes, Long Islands come in a bottle," I said laughing out loud to Nikki, my Bunkie, as I am dwelling on the fact that it's a popular drink when going out to night clubs or parties.

"Girl you is crazy! Ain't that just like the Friday's kind?" she asked.

I laughed, "Yeah but I think it's a lot stronger than Friday's. It creeps up on you. It's got a lot of liquors in it. Probably smoother than Fridays too. It's well blended."

"Oh ok girl. I seen it but never had it drinking. Ain't my cup of tea anyway. Now if you asked about rellos I can school yo young ass," Nicki smirked and said.

"I know you could," I said. I looked over at the window as I remembered where I paused at to finish my story.

So the lady gave me my change back at the same window with my Long Island. I count it and notice it's a dollar short. I then asked if the price had changed or went up because it was a dollar less the week before. I'm sitting there at the window thinking to myself, 'it's only a dollar'. She snaps – she as in the lady at the window. She yells with a thick ass accent, maybe Korean or some Asian language 'No, NO No dolla' mo' Dis' ma price you nigga bitch.' All hostile and abrupt. I was truly caught off guard. I just stared at her dead in the eye like I can't believe you. Alarming to the tenth degree, I state to her, 'Don't get mad at me and call me names. I'm your customer and not your employee. It was a man with brown hair that sold it to me last week'. She comes back with, "No you lie whateva!" I apologetically gave my, 'okay' as she rolled her eyes, and griped the glass window.

She glared at me with a hateful look in her eyes and said, "You want money back?" I shook my head no and explained that wasn't the problem. It was her disrespect. She goes on to disrespect again "then leave nigga' bitch," and slams the window shut. Appalled at the situation ,my thoughts kick into gear as fast as the speed of lighting. The right side said, 'just go, she just not happy'. The left side states the most obvious, 'you didn't disrespect her. You need an apology. You know what I do.' I then loop around to the front of the store where the entrance is located, take a look in the mirror, and tell the girls that I will be right back. Shelly asks, 'what are you about to go and do?' I look her right in the eye and tell her, 'Get an apology.' As I walked into the front door of the store, I realized it wasn't worth the effort but also knew those girls in the truck might demand respect one day if they are faced with an opportunity to receive it. Hell, I'll tell them in a heartbeat to receive it however they can get it. I made up my mind. Bright lights, no other customers. Just the cashier behind the register looking content . The calm before the storm.

"Excuse me, where is the lady who was at the window?" I asked very calmly and almost innocent like.

"Oh the boss? She's in her office." He pointed and I walked in that direction.

"Thanks."

As she sat staring angrily at her computer screen, I asked her, "Can I speak with you for a minute?"

"No, bout what?" She said in her broken English.

"Well, you owe me an apology because you disrespected me, and I did nothing to disrespect you."

"No, no apologize to you. Leave my store now or I call police."

"No, I will leave when the police get here."

As the tug of words continued, there was a point when this lady grabbed the telephone and puts it about an inch close to my nose. She did that right after she threw money at me and said, 'that why you came. Now leave!" The charade game continued, and the girls walked into the store. I later found out that a man that came in who witnessed the incident went to the car and told the girls it looked like it was about to go down. I forfeited all ties to winning this word game when she said, ‘all three nigga bitches get out my store.’ Now lost in translation, I came to demand some form of an apology, but had just been disrespected again. Worse, this time all three of us got disrespected. That part hurt my ego. I thought to myself, ‘it is now time to do something.’ And something, I did do. Shelves got knocked over. A $4.29 bag of Doritos, Lays, Planter peanuts, gummies, bean dips, jalapeno cheeses, assortments of Chex Mix, Skittles, and Snickers all hit the ground tumbling.

“What do you mean?” asked my Bunkie.

“I knocked all of the stuff on the floor. I knocked more shelves over, and more stuff fell. I just wanted her to have to clean it up.”

“But you should have just left,” said Nikki.

“I know I should have but when you are enraged and disrespected, it sometimes calls for a scene of disaster. Especially if you and your significant other just got into it.”

Nikki was enjoying the story. "So anyways what happened?"

Well, we ran out of the store. The birthday girl, my god-daughter, and then me, all of us ran to the car. I was the one driving, the birthday girl was in the passenger seat, and my god-daughter was behind the passenger seat. Next I hear Shelly yell, "You not getting in bitch!" Shelly was holding the lock down to the car door.

"Wait, who not getting in? The lady from the store? What she ran out after y'all did or something?" my Bunkie asked me with a clear look of confusion spread across her face.

"Girl yea' that's exactly what she did. I knew she was behind me but didn't know that she had the nerve to touch the car door handle until Shelly was telling her to let it go."

"So y'all could have beat her ass and did whatever y'all wanted to because she didn't give a damn about her life at the point in time. Shit I don't think y'all would have been in the wrong either if y'all did beat her ass. Shit, now you got me mad thinking about the whole situation." Nikki was clearly more irritated than confused stated.

"Right, girl that ain't the half of it. There's more to come."

My God daughter yelled, "Pull off God mom she not getting in this car." She said it but I was already thinking it. The car was already started. I thought it was going to be a breeze to get the apology, but I thought wrong. Foot on the gas pedal reversing as if I'm driving in the Daytona 500, we screeched on out of the parking lot at the speed of lighting. The girls looked back and Reign asked where the lady was. I looked in the rearview and told her I didn't know that she'd probably went back in and called the police. Fast forward to 8:30 am Saturday morning. My phone rang and I had numerous new messages, voicemails, texts, Facebook notifications, the whole bit. Damn near every line of communication was visited. One message in particular scared the living day lights out of me it said: RENDI U DAMN NEAR KILDT A LADY, SHE N CRITICAL CONDITION. SHE HAS BLEEDING ON HER BRAIN, PELVIS BROKEN, ANKLE

FRACTURE, RIB FRACTURE, 2 BROKEN RIBS. WHAT THE FUCK DID U DO!!!!!?????? Dazed, confused, scared shitless, panicked. I didn't know what to do.

"Wait did they come and get you?"

"No I turned myself in and retained a lawyer."

"What did they charge you with?"

"Reckless driving, malicious destruction of property, and failure to stop at the scene of an accident. I plead to leaving the scene, so they dropped the rest."

"Damn that carry time huh?"

"Getting to that part now."

3 Months later

As I walk into the court room for sentencing. I see three news stations, a journalist, and the judge. I am terrified. I thought the TV stuff was over. I'm first to go in front of the judge.

He states, "Have you ever heard of the old adage sticks and stones will break my bones, but words will never hurt me?" I reply, "yes."

"Well you should have listened. I don't think you are a good fit for probation. I sentence you to the top of your guidelines. Bailiff, take her."

Distraught is all I remember from the rest of that day. It passed like a blur. Three-hundred-thirty-six hours later, my story was told numerous times to a variety of people who asked.

After a month or so of serving my sentence, I see a familiar face. It's a cousin of mine. She asks me if anyone had been up to the jail to come and see me I tell her no.

"Where Aunt Brenda at?" She asked me.

"I don't know. Probably at home not thinking about me. You know I'm the black sheep of the family."

Don't think like that." She responds. "Take this time to reflect. To get the anger off of my heart." I replied, " Yeah. I hear you cuz."

As the weeks go by, my cousin and I start to build a stronger bond. I begin opening up about my background. More than what she knew.

"Man cuz, reach out to your parents" she says.

"Naw forget them, they know where I'm at."

The night before it was my cousin's release date. She came to me and asked if I had written a letter to my parents.

"I'm bout to leave cuz. Did you write it yet?"

"Girl naw, I told you I'm not tryna do that. So they can read it find no fault and still look at me as if everything is all my fault. I'm good. It's just gonna make me look like an ass to think they will ever respond or look my way when I get out. But anyways come play cards your last night."

"Alright, but only if you write that letter to your parents."

"Bet." It was done. I said I was going to do something, so I had to be a woman and stick to my word.

Finding the words to express the hurt, anger, resentment, pain, abandonment, deception, came not too easy. I lost sleep and cried my eyes out trying to put it all together. But in the end, my letter was written.

"Did you receive a response back?" Nikki my Bunkie asked.

"No. I did it knowing that it would never get acknowledged or spoken on again. It actually helped me out. It was very therapeutic. It was like having your first heartbreak again but with a form of closure. As, a matter of fact can you think of a time when you received your first heart break?"

"Yea, it was when my mom had died......."

"Nikki write it down, try and get some closure from it."

" Rendi, that's deep!"

"Girl, I know. Shit I'm deep, but not as deep as the scars that an unresolved emotional heartbreak can leave."

Story #1: Looking at You Daily

Looking at your faces day to day

Wishing I could take this pain away

Memories of you going through my mind

It never stops… just feels like its constant rewind

Every night before I close my eyes

I think about all of my white lies

I am so sorry another time in here

I'm very thankful just not another year

Nightly I stare at you guys

Wishing this was just another dreamin disguise

Hoping to wake up next to you

And be done playing this charades game too

After this is all over

I will never forget the words "Roren"

I am so ready for the day

I can again see you face to face

And never again want my own space

Story# 2: 2008

So I travel back into a particular time in my life of substance abuse and an extra mix of poison. I only remember a bottle of pain pills sitting on the counter that deemed to be three times the size it really was. Consuming them all and living to tell the best part…. The glory in life is the Angel that stood above me after days of healing, telling me these simple nine words, "You need to find out your purpose in life, Kelly you are a miracle."

Story #3: Our Family

We are never weak.

We are very strong

We are never wrong

But our family grows forever long

And forever us belong

We as a family will always seek the path

We will always live daily in our wrath

We will never forget where our love comes from

Never abuse nor some

We are a family that comes in different kind

You will never know, what is going thru our minds

But no matter where we go

Us family will always be found toe to toe

We are never weak

We are very strong

"Our family sticks are forever long!"

Story #4: "Strong Enough"

Those that don't know me, I am a fighter

And I will fight until it's over

B3 no class or me, still mini deputy

I tried, I tried to stick, stay, but may have to now go away

Not for long

But they did play me wrong… like a war

I did put it upon you kids with a swore

Not good enough

Those bitches all just thought they were tough

This time I tried, and yet haven't lied

All these ppl know me

Their just hating you see

So like I said if I end up in the hole

Just remember I tried playing my role

Only you kids know

You know I'm not cut like no hoe

I hope you all realize

With my experience you'll think wise

Know all bitches are fake

They all are snakes

Maybe one day they'll all awake

I will die trying, never lying

Story #5: My First Heartbreak Came in the Form of an Identity Crisis

You pronounce it " Ah-rain- yah".

"What how? "

"The D is silent!"

Yes, all of my younger years I had to explain the saying and also the spelling of my first name. Being adopted and not necessarily being in tune with my roots made it hard for me to identify with my name vs. my given names. I was brought up being called "Rainya/ Arainya. But my true name is spelled Arendia. Which is pronounced " Ah-Ren-DI-Ah". At the age of 18 I was so tired of explaining how to match the pronunciation with how it was said I gave myself a new nick name. Ren-di. Or short form Ren. I was told plenty of times "oh that's beautiful, what does it mean?" I had no idea. So I prayed on and I got led to the meaning "is favored."

Story #6: Shamara

Well I can say it all started by the age of 12. I started looking for love in all the wrong places and I guess you can say "I found it!" I am the baby of six girls, and I grew up in a fatherless home. I always thought I was wise beyond my years, so I thought I could handle what "Big Girl" territory bought. I became pregnant at the age of 12 and gave birth at 13. My so called first "love" who was the same age as me, denied it was all good when I gave up the goods, but when the going got tough, he kept it moving! My heart was torn into pieces, only behind closed doors because I wanted to keep up this image that no one or nothing could hurt me! So the year of "97" and I entered High School, Brandon was 1 years old, and I thought I had it all together!! My mind was in my books and I felt in charge of my heart again. February of 98: comes and I met the most handsome, charming young man eve! This(gentleman) swept me off my feet! He knew what to say and just how to say it! All along he was a monster in disguise! He beat me for 11 years from the time I was 14 until I was a 25 years old. I bore 5 of his children and buried one as well due to domestic violence I went in labor early with him and our daughter Shanica (our 3rd Child). But there is always light at the end of the tunnel, God rescued me and showed me all the love I need! Through Christ I learned to love myself and others with the love of God and also that I am a conqueror not a victim anymore!!!

Story #7: Brandy

"I don't know how to tell you kids this, but your mother just expired," my grandfather's baritone voice let out as he walked across the dining room in his and my grandmother's city flat. He hung up the phone just moments earlier with the hospital. I sunk into the old large sofa and looked across the room to my small brother sitting on the other couch. His face turned bright red. He held his breath, and tears started drenching his chubby cheeks. That was my cue to play big sister. I leapt up off the couch and embraced him with my whole upper body. "It will be ok. I promise it will be ok. Don't be sad. We will be ok." His tears drenched my shoulder. I didn't cry. He was a month from turning 13, and I was 14.

My mother's death was the most tragic thing I've ever experienced. Throughout most of my young life with her we fought. There was little love expressed between the two of us. Aside from a handful of random memories when I was too small to really notice, most of my memories of her are filled with anger, tension, resentment, and a very sad woman. She rarely smiled, except when she was with a few selected friends getting high. She hated my father. She would cheat on him regularly and would bring me, my brother, and my sister as accomplices. Often we were left alone in some strangers' living room while she escaped behind closed doors to emerge with a laugh and a smile. I could never make her smile the way her special "private" friends and drugs could. I would do everything she asked me to, and it was never enough. I could "always do better" she would say. And deep down, I knew I could too.

Sometimes she would cry alone in her room, for hours on end. I would sheepishly knock on her bedroom door and ask what was wrong. She'd tell me to go away, or even be honest to tell me she wanted to die and wanted to kill herself. I didn't understand why we weren't enough for her to live for or make her happy. So I would keep trying.

As we got older, my sister became more rebellious. She was always getting reprimanded at school. My mom and her developed a very tight bond and would do a lot of things together. My sister began to torment me, and my mother would always defend her. She always blamed it on my sister being mixed race and I had it easy because I was white with blonde hair and blue eyes.

Over time I learned to stay closer to my dad. Despite his tumultuous and abusive relationship with my mother, he was a loyal and tender father. He tried to spoil me, because he didn't disagree with my cries that my mother didn't love me. We'd go for long drives and listen to music or take trips into the city to my grandmother's house where I'd cry over my mother being so mean and hurtful, her wicked physical abuse, and her cold and unloving nature. My grandmother would hug me and share that her mother didn't love her either. "If only I could do better," I kept thinking. No matter how much my dad loved and spoiled me, and my grandmother related to me. I craved my mother's love and recognition more than anything.

Middle school approached and hormones set in… My sister became more and more rebellious, my brother immersed himself in sports, and my father fell further and further into his depression. He had given in and went to rehab, making promises to my mother and breaking them. She continued cheating, lying, crying, and was always high. I learned to hide in my bedroom when she was home and timed my day according to her schedule to avoid her. If I ever crossed her path, I said few words, and she would snicker and make degrading comments. But I still did all I could. I received straight A's in school, won all awards, was captain of all my sports teams, and was the president of as many clubs as I could sign up for. My bedroom wall was covered with certificates. None of it mattered. I didn't exist. And when I did, I was her verbal and physical punching bag.

I would journal nightly my rage and hurt over my mom and my sister. They ganged up on me and I never could understand why I couldn't earn her love despite all my work being her perfect child. My sister, the trouble- maker and rebel, got all the attention and forgiveness. I was a shadow. And I was angry, sad, and lonely.

One day, sitting on the toilet, my mother called me in and told me she understood why I hated her. I told her I didn't. She said she knew I did, and didn't blame me, because she hated her mother too. I trembled when she talked to me, never knowing if what I said would be right or wrong, and I wanted to yell to her "why don't you love me? I'm a kid! I don't hate you. I want to love you," but I couldn't. She told me that she thought her, and I were a lot alike, and that is why we didn't like each other. She said that when I got older, I'd understand her better, and we might get along better. So that is what I did, I decided to focus on the future, forget about my childhood, and obsess about being an adult with an adult life, so then, finally, I could have my mother, and her acceptance, approval, and love for me. We could have what her and my sister had, but better.

I decided I wanted to be an architect, so I could build and design her ideal house. We were poor and lived in a trailer. My mom always complained and cried about not having enough money. That we shouldn't live in a trailer. So I'd make a bunch of money, give it to her and buy her whatever she wanted, and design and build her dream house. I sketched all the time. I fantasized about big, fancy colleges, and being successful. I wouldn't be what her and my dad were. Not ever.

When she suddenly died in the winter of my freshman year of high school, my heart broke into a million tiny pieces. Shattered. I stared blankly at the TV screen as they played my mom's story over and over again on the news. "Tragedy", they all called it. Was it? Was it an accident she was high and walked out into the middle of the semi- frozen lake and fell through? She spoke of death constantly. Was she finally free? Free of her suffering, free of being my mom?

As I walked into the waiting room of the hospital, a large group of people looked up and stared at us, holding their breath.

All I could mutter was “I need to see my mom.” “Honey you can’t,” my aunt said. “ I have to I need to talk to her.” “But she’s not in good shape.” She was already dead. She died before they pulled her in from the frozen lake. I looked firmly back at my aunt. “I need to see her. I have to tell her something!” Her eyes filled up. She walked across the room to the nurse, and then hurried me over.

They walked my brother and I into the sterile room, my aunt holding my hand, my dad holding my brothers. My uncle, already in the room, crying. Tubes came out of multiple parts of her body, and she covered the entire bed. She was a larger woman, but water had filled her body so much, she was swollen and unrecognizable. I'll never forget that image. I laid myself across her stomach with my arms stretched out across her stomach with my arms stretched out across her and all I could repeat was, “I'm so sorry. I'm so sorry we didn't get along. I'm so sorry I didn’t make your dreams come true.” I began to wail. The room filled up with tears and that's when my aunt grabbed me and said it was time to go. I told her I wasn't done yet. She said she knew but the doctors needed the room.

Just like that, my plan was over. I'd never be able to win her love and attention. I never got the chance. I never got the chance to get those warm hugs, gentle kisses, the "its ok," the pats on the back, the security of knowing I was ok and accepted. That I was enough.

Every day since, I've struggled with alcohol addiction, infidelity, toxic friendships and relationships, issues with money, self- worth, and my identity. My youth was spent trying to prove myself and win my mother's love and becoming something I thought she wanted. When she died, although she was gone in the physical sense, the programming within me remained. I spent all of my high school years, college and well into my 30's trying to prove myself and be something worthy of love. But it was never enough. I hated myself I hated the person I was obsessed at becoming, and I hated that I couldn't even be perfect enough at mastering this shell and facade I wanted so badly to be.

As I slowly begun to embrace the breakdown, the unraveling, the imperfections, and the beauty in the mess, the self-acceptance takes place. The beauty and the love is in the mess, not the unattainable perfection. I don't know if we'd be friends. I don't know if she'd be proud of me or not. It's one of the mysteries I'll have to live with forever. But in the meantime, I'm learning to love and be friends with myself.

Story #8: My Aunt

Well starting today was about the biggest slap in the face ever. I had got news from my loving sister that my aunt that I love so much had passed away while I have been in here incarcerated for about 4 months. Now I have been waiting for these people to give me any new news that (will tell me what) I will be going through. Drug court soon the guy had told me that he will be seeing me Monday, which it is Monday now and no word from him yet. It's crazy because I am here and it's like 6:30 pm and nothing yet. And I am so stressed out, I'm lost, lonely, worried scared, sad, angry, and not able to do anything. Like my hands are tied behind my back and someone just keeps punching me in my stomach. I had to argue with my ex-husband again. Just to put something in my account. When the bastard owes me everything in this world its pathetic he can manipulate me and abuse me. And able to get away with it and still able to talk to me with Disrespect and able to even raise his voice to me. But on top of all that, still not able to even pray over my aunt. She was the sweetest person ever she told it how it was and didn't care if she told the truth as long as it was the truth. She cared for others so much and she had so much love and her poor cats will miss her dearly. She loved them so much. If I were there I would be able to fix some of the things that she needed to be fixed. Thank God that I still have faith in Him and that will never stop. I just hope the best for tomorrow and believe I will be able to stay strong. I am sober and that is the best thing that I have now and my relationship with God, it's such a blessing but I will miss my Aunt dearly, and I pray that they don't hurt her cats because that's what she loved so dearly. I have Faith that I will hear soon but now that my aunt is gone, I'm so lost and alone but not ready. I know God is beside me each and every day, but it won't be the same anymore. I still plan to stay sober and focused to stay strong and I believe that things will be better or if, they are getting worst it doesn't mean I will lose my faith.

I will stay sober and focused, and it is going to be a little bit of a challenge. But I have Faith in every day, and I plan not to worry about tomorrow but let tomorrow worry for itself. Well I hope one day I will be able to be an inspiration to someone that needs a shoulder. I need to appreciate life and appreciate every breath I still have in my body. But I will keep my head up and move through with all that God has for me. Thank you for hearing my story for what it is, and I have learned from it too. I just need a shoulder or an act that someone cares at this moment.

Story #9: Pain is Love

I have had many heartbreaks throughout my life. My first hardest heartbreak happened when I was 23 years old and lasted as long as 7 plus years, until I was almost 31 years old. During that period of time I went through a lot of changes mentally and physically. It was like "pain is Love". Which in the end I believe made me a better, stronger, spiritual, and conscious person. But first was my actions. At 23 years old I had everything I could ever want. House, new car, my girl, our son, money, clothes, and travel to different places whenever I wanted. I loved the life I lived, and the heart of it was spent in the street to provide for this lifestyle. Thinking I was making my family happy when I should have just been there doing the right things to provide for our needs. But they never knew all the chances I was taking for my money. I was young, naive and only thinking of myself.

My thinking is 23 ways to get money every hour of the day by any means possible. Not really realizing the hurt and pain that I was causing my family with my mind set. All it took was one bad night, one bad hour, from many bad decisions that led me astray. And that night was when I helped pull an armed robbery. No it wasn’t my first and I wasn't hurting for money. But it was my last armed robbery that put me in prison. I have never been locked up no more than a few days and now I am facing years in prison. As I sit in that cell handcuffed all I could think of was my son and how I let him down as a father. Yes , I cried. But my tears couldn’t save me. Before all of this would spend every day together playing going on car rides visiting friends and family. Now in less than a day dad is gone for years and years. While I was locked up and away. I would hear stories about how my son would wait at the front door or stare out the window looking for his dad to come home. In prison I would try to run from this pain by not calling anyone for long periods of time. Plus, I would work out until my muscles hurt causing pain to myself. Day after day, year after year I would chase physical pain away from the mental pain. It was my outlet. A way to live without love from my family. Because I felt powerless to help or do anything. When my son would come to visit me while I was in prison, it was heartbreaking to see him come and go. He would tell me, ‘Dad I’ma get you out of here.’ He was so passionate in his eyes about getting me out I could not even respond. He was growing without me. I was not there to see it and give him my love for so many years. I remember sitting outside or in my room imagining that me and my son were out having fun at a park or a beach. I would find me laughing at myself sometimes. Then a fight would break out and someone was stabbed and then I was back to reality that I was stuck in prison where there’s no love with more years to go. There were days I felt like giving up. I was gone for so long that I felt like I would never get out of that place. It was like trying to live life in a coffin. On my visit with my son I told him, “Words cannot express how bad I feel for not being there with you son” Then he hit me with these words that put me back on focus whenever I felt down and out. He told me, “Dad, I'm not mad at you because I Love You.'' those words coming from my 5-year-old son still sticks to me till this very day. I live off these words every time before I do anything that can get me years in prison.

Story #10

All my life I've been the problem child. I never fail being in jail, pregnant at 16 not finishing school can't keep a job, just not doing anything right. Hear my story…. I had a wonderful childhood my mom worked hours to provide for hers. Dad was in and out when I was about 7 or 10 that age a little blurry. He was drugged out he was my first heartbreak, but he wasn't my last. The father of my child left me hurt, confused, bruised, burned, basically DEAD. My heart longed for him I put him first. Every relationship starts off great just like this one, he said he loved me, I was his one and only he said he waited for me I was 15-years-old old he was 18-years-old. We, well I waited till was 16-years-old to have sex with him the day I turned 1yrs old he asked me to have his child and I was in love with him that I gave in I wasn't thinking about my life I wanted to make him happy I didn't want him to leave me, I thought he was going to be a great dad Never be like mines. I said yes I'll have your child I told him everything gave him all of me and soon as he knew he had me right where he wanted me it was

DONE. I was holding my first child at 16-years-old and wasn't due till November 15th I found out I was pregnant April 8th I was in love so nobody opinion matter but his He started being abusive and slapping me punching me I was 6 months. He punched me in my chest and kicked me out of his house with a bloody nose.

Story #11 Mindy

My name is Mindy, and this is my story. It will be a short version cause the long version is just too much.

Also, I'm not sure that doing this ,what feelings will evolve that I'm afraid of all over again. I had a great upbring. I went to church, my family didn't fight, or drink or do drugs , they were very strict with me. A white picket fence family, I met my husband who is the father of my 3 sons. We were married for 13 years, I had feelings he was cheating and doing things he shouldn't, but who wants to believe that when you think life is great and you now have your own white picket fence ,or so you think . The last straw was probably the 10th girl (who range in age 18 to 51) I was pregnant with my 3rd son 7 months along, when I found out I was so distraught. I couldn't figure out what was wrong with me. I figured it was time to put my foot down ,no more games between us ,no more lies , I divorced the man I thought was the love of my life . I remember just crying all day ,every day. I had already had my son ,so I started drinking a lot .

Not remembering why I was waking up in bed next to my parents with swollen eyes again from drinking and crying all night. I was so disgusted in myself . I had this quilt for myself I didn't deserve . I dealt with him for as long as I did and that was nothing but my fault I needed to man up and stop crying and drinking and take care of my kids , I struggled, it was hard ,I was discouraged that I couldn't do better for my kids . Life went on, I picked myself up off the ground more times than I can count. I eventually ran into my high school sweetheart. In high school he was sweet, he was " that man" but it was school, and we were just kids. He and I started to date again. We went on dating for a couple years. He moved in and we built a life together. He was great with my kids. He and my ex got along great. Co-parenting worked well.

I was excited, happy, in love and I was on top of the world. Something I said I would never ever do again… I married him. Another huge, beautiful wedding. Life was perfect. A while into our marriage pain pills turned into drugs. Hard core drugs. Our relationship started to fuse, not romantically anymore but verbally.

Mental abuse, emotional abuse and then came the physical. When there weren't enough drugs it was my fault, I was always hiding something from him he thought.

He's 3x's bigger than me. I was and still am very intimidated by him. I make sure to this day he has no idea where I reside. The days got longer, and we got higher. I gave my kids to their dad a lot more than was ok. I was worthless. I was getting my ass beat daily. Learning to like the taste of my own blood. Going to bed at night dreaming about my own coffin colors, waking up crying cause my kids weren't even crying at their own mother's funeral. I was on my hands and knees with my heart on the ground begging and praying for my life, even though I felt I didn't deserve any bit of it. I was willing to beg for my fake white picket fence life back. I was willing to live fake, betrayed, and unloved. But it's hard to leave someone you think you love so much. And really to be honest, I feel I really do love him still. I feel he was my soul mate. There are a lot of parts to this story that I left out that I just can't write about. Like when in 2014 he tried to kill me with a car.

I can't actually write it all down and do it and feel it all over again right now. I'm sorry for that.

But in the end of all this, My feelings and my feelings today are numb. I hope that all these feelings don't leave me numb to a lot of situations forever.

By the way I am divorced now, and he fought it hard, begged to change. I almost at one point regret it. Regret isn't' a good feeling along with numbness. Regret and numbness= lonely. I hope i don't feel that forever.

Story #12: A Heartbreak in High School

It was a normal Spring day in 1991. My brother and I had gone to school like we always did. I was 15 and a sophomore in high school.

We returned home around 3pm and finished our chores. I was on the corded phone we had in the kitchen on the wall. When my father returned home from work. He proceeded to his favorite lazy boy in front of the TV like he had to years prior to that day. I made him some food and served it to him in his chair and then proceeded to get back on the phone, as teenage girls do. My father wanted me to take care of his plate. I said I would after I got off the phone. He proceeded to get up, threw me up against the wall.

A little while later after my brother and father fought. I called my mother at work and told her what happened.

After 27 years of marriage, that incident made my mother divorce my father.

He never really did recover from the divorce. My brother and I were also never the same after being uprooted halfway through our sophomore year of high school.

I have always wondered where we would be, had I just did what he asked that day.

My father never loved anybody else, he said that my mother was the only woman he ever loved, all the way til the day he died. Had I reacted differently, would he still be here? Would my mother still be alone as she never dated anyone else as well.

Things I will never know and live with every day.

Story #13

I grew up fast. Met my husband at the age of 17, pregnant by 18 and gave birth to my baby girl at the age of 19. It was love at first sight, married by the age of 22. We went to Vegas and got married. It was awesome had family and friends go with us; we had the time of our lives. Me and my husband were living the good life. Both had good jobs, 2 cars, went to football games and concerts all the time. We had a wonderful marriage.

Four years into our marriage me and my husband decided to have one more kid. We got pregnant with twins, and on Sept 1st we had 2 tiny baby boys. Life was complete so I thought. I started to notice that my husband wasn't himself after the twins were born. He wasn't home a lot. I started to notice that he was spending money that he could not explain, where he spent it. He wasn't so good to me anymore like he used to be emotionally or physically. One of our friends said that they thought he was using hard drugs. My first thoughts were, "No way, he would never do that-and hide it from me." So being the women that I am, I started to snoop on him. Go through his things and found proof that he was. I asked him about it, and he told me the truth.

I told him he needed to get help or leave… not going to have that around our kids. So he chose to leave. Left me with a 7 yr old and 2 babies. To top it all off when he left me, he went to a girl that he had been cheating on me with. When I found out about her once again, I asked him, and he said that he had been cheating on me with her for a while. In that moment, my heart fell out of my chest. Broken into pieces. Never had I ever thought that he would do that. That was the first time I had my heart broken.

Story #14: It's Me

My story is pretty simple, at least compared to others. Writing this makes me feel self- righteous and that's a feeling I do not like. However I need to keep in mind that hopefully these words help others. To sum up what has affected me the most is easy - ME. It's all about me. It always has been. I never knew how selfish I am until I went to jail for the third time for drunk driving.

I was arrested off the end of a very long night. I worked my 12-hour shift and went to two local bars where I knew the bartenders. I was with my ex-girlfriend and we were of course drunk. My ex is a full-blown alcoholic so being around her is hard not to drink. Leaving the second bar at 3 am, she begged me not to drive. I of course told her I can do whatever I want. I never took anyone's opinion or well-fare into consideration.

I hurt so many people by my actions. I was of course arrested. And in turn created a whirlwind of emotions for the first time I realized that I was my worst enemy. I learned to love myself thru this process and put others above me. I do not need my old self anymore. Thinking of others first has given me all the fulfillment I need.

Story #15: Best Mom

There was once this beautiful young mom. She was all alone in a foreign city known for making cars. She was 19 with her first band new baby girl and they lived in a rundown trailer, her very own first place as a grown Mother. It was December and all she could worry about was if the newborn daughter was warm enough, without heat and a blizzard outside. She would layer blankets on the crib mattress and line the walls of it with blankets, tape her in her best blanket and then cover the top of the crib w/ blankets. Her baby seemed so warm and content and so amazing and beautiful. The young mom was so proud of the life she created and the changes she was making to be the best mother she could be. So many hopes, plans, and dreams filled her head whenever she held her baby, so much love..

The young mother did not have a relationship w/ her own parents since she'd left an argument 3 years ago. However now that her baby was 1yr she wanted her daughter to know her grandparents, and they were excited to meet there new granddaughter. To the mom's surprise, her parents neglected her baby! The grand rapids were furious that her daughter was of color! The young mother was so hurt by their reaction, she cursed them and vowed to never speak to them again! How could they be so evil to deny my beautiful bay? Don't they see my eyes? They must not love me either!" either she thought.

2 years passed and her baby grew happy healthy and bright as a star! The mother was in bless whenever she looked at her baby. She worked very hard to support them both and her daughter would go to her father's house while she was working. One day when they returned home...she gave her baby now 3 years old, a bath before bed, when she noticed a stench and some discharge! She took her to her doctor the next day and they ran some test." What could be wrong with my baby? She thought. Maybe an allergic reaction to the soap she used.

But when the doctor came back with results and a few other people, she knew something was wrong. The doctor then said, "I'm afraid to say that these people are from Child Protective

Service. Your daughters test came back positive for semen. Your daughters test came back for Chlamydia." She was so confused! Words couldn't express her thoughts but lost for words.

Many years of therapy, court, and heartache followed, well into her baby's adult years with her grandparents right beside her, and her Father God carrying them all along the way.

Story #16: Lauren

Hi, I'm Lauren. Usually when girls talk about their first heartbreak, it's about some boy who promised to give them the world but left them with nothing. Well mine is not quite the usual heartbreak. My first heartbreak was given to me by my mother. Daughters are supposed to feel loved, protected, happy, supported, guided, and so much more by their Mothers. But I felt none of that by mine. What I felt was abandonment, unsafe, depressed, unloved, and alone. Drugs, money, and men are what my mom chose to love. My brother and I grew up thinking having a mom coming and going as she pleases and leaving us with random people was normal. Well it's not. If It wasn't for my brother, I may not have even been here today. Fun family nights with mom consisted of going to the bar, sitting, and watching her have fun. Sometimes, we got to play pool or some other game. But mostly we walked off and would go outside and go on adventures. By the time my mom even noticed my brother and I were gone, it would have been too late.

One time Nick and I got bored and walked off outside. There were train tracks on the side of the bar. We decided to go walk on the and get away from all the drunk adults. We got pretty far down the tracks and came up to a small manmade lake. We started picking up small rocks and throwing them in the lake. Nick turned around and saw someone walking towards us. So he grabbed my arm and was looking around. We knew he was looking for us. He was the same guy sitting alone in the bar. He had followed us. Nick and I sat still until he continued walking. When we couldn't see him any more we came out of the bushes and started walking fast back to the bar. The train tracks were about twenty or so feet above the lake. So we were trying to be careful, but we heard the guy yell at us. So we started to run. I tripped and fell 20 feet down into the water. I smacked my head on something in the water and got knocked out. My brother I guess ran down the side of the tracks and jumped into the water and grabbed me. Once my brother pulled me out of the water, the man who followed us, picked me up. He took me back to the bar and Nick followed. I guess my mom had sent him, instead of getting us herself. He walked in with us, and I started to wake up in my mom's lap, while she was taking care of my head wound in the bathroom. The guy ended up taking us all home. My mom seemed more angry than worried. She asked why we wandered off, and we said because it's not fun to be around drunk adults. Not much was said after that. That is just one of many bad incidents that were caused by my mom not caring enough. But we were blessed with an amazing dad. I'm thankful to have him. If it weren't for my mom, I wouldn't be who I am today. I am strong and know what not to do as a mother.

Story #17: Jamie

Friends and Family

Friends and family are why we are here

Keep the ones you love near,

Friends I love you so much,

You are all part of me,

That no one can touch,

A lot of what I say and do,

In a lot of way reflects on you,

You are there for me,

When no one else could be,

I love you all for that,

I even tip my hat,

Time goes so fast,

But our love is what makes it last,

I hope to have you all forever,

Through fights, money or whatever,

We all have a lot of fun,

When all is said and done

Story #18: Adrienne

I remember when I first got my heart broken I was 16 and just had my first child.

My sons' father and I got along just fine until I had my son that's when he started beating on me and started staying out all the times of the night I remember sitting wondering what I did wrong to deserve that kind of treatment I couldn't figure out what so all I could do was cry day in and day out and still never understood why. Because of his wrongdoing I had no trust in men for a very long time because I felt unworthy of love I felt as if no one could or would love me I was 16 no job no education and a baby with nothing when he left me I felt as I couldn't go on.

I thought I would die for sure cause I turned by back on everyone to please him, so I had no

Friends so not only did I feel lonely I was lonely, and it hurt cause I had no one to talk to about the heart ache I was feeling it was feeling that i can't imagine feeling again.

Story #19: Life Now

Things aren't what they were,

Feel like I got kicked in the ass with a spur,

This path to gettin clean,

Is surely motherfucken mean,

I'm doin all I possibly can,

I almost grabbed my shit and ran,

I feel empty in a lot of ways,

But with these boys is,

Where my heart lay's,

All the people around me are in awe,

Because they remember that they saw,

I'm a different person now,

I look in the mirror and I'm

Straight up like, WOW

My mind is in a different place,

Tryin to make our kids proud,

Screaming I'm fucking sober out loud!!

Story #20: My Child

I've had many heartbreaks! One that stands out the most is when my ex took our child out of my life because we had a fight WE got into. The little girl wasn't mine biologically - but I loved her like she was. For a while I couldn't even think of her w/o breaking out in tears. I couldn't listen to certain songs or even speak her name (which is the same as mine- with "ll" in the front if it.) My ex was and still is very vindictive, extremely! Because I didn't want to be with and pursue her to reconcile me and the child had to suffer for it. It was a sad time for me.

In all fairness I will admit- I was not a saint in this relationship. I seriously can't stand my ex, however, because I still love that child- I will always keep the chore if she is in need. Love is amazing.

Story #21: Middle School Clique

One of the true first heartbreaks that I can recall is when I was in middle school. I was always a leader, confident, and liked myself till seventh grade. Due to being a mere 25 pounds overweight, I was made fun of by my peers. I was called fat, ugly, a whale, and Shamoo amongst many other names. Kids were evil and played jokes, games, and pranks, not only behind my back, but to my face. I felt anxious a lot due to this, so my social life became a huge trigger for anxiety. I still chose to feel accepted, with popular and lied, so I did anything I had to do to keep them as friends and in the "clique" w/ them. The emotions I felt during and thru all of this can be described as; confused, defenseless, degraded, didn't measure up, embarrassed, fear, humiliated, hurt, crushed, vulnerable, rejected, mistreated, lost and insecure.

Luckily, by the grace and love of God, I do not let this affect me today and love myself. I have grown stronger, know my identity in Christ, and used this to make me into the amazing woman I am today. In sum, this is one of the first major "heartbreaks" I encountered in my life.

Story #22: Christen

My first love I met when I was 12. I was with him until he got murdered. I was 21, I've never recovered from this. My life has spiraled out of control since. My heart still aches when I think of him.

Story #23: Domini

My name is Domini. I am a 34-year-old female, born in Gary Indiana. The very first time a piece of my heart was broken. I was 3 years old still living in Gary, IN. My family was at my Grandma house. I don't remember why, family dinner, or my grandma was watching us? Not sure, but N-E way. My Grandma owned a little ranch style home, and in her house, she had a very big, finished basement that had a room in the back that her adopted boys used as a bedroom.

One of those boys took me into that room. I vaguely remember him getting me to get in the bed with him. I remember him putting his penis in my face and asking me to suck on it. I remember it barely fitting in my mouth. How it was hard, and I almost choked on it. I remember how he had my head under the covers as he lay on the bed. I also remember how someone walked in, still till this day I do not know who it was, if they knew I was there or not, but they did what they had to do, said what they had to say and left. Meanwhile he was pushing down on my head so hard that I could hardly breath, I felt like I was suffocating, I couldn't move, speak, scream, I couldn't even swallow. After whoever it was left. He resumed action as if nothing ever happened.

I never knew that what was happening was wrong. I don't even remember if that was the first time, last time, if it went on for years, if it lasted for minutes or hours.

I do know that this man, boy at the time that did this was someone that I trusted, my mom trusted, my grandmother trusted. I blocked it out for most of my life, I tried to live a normal life, but as I got older I started doing things that I knew weren't right. I didn't even tell my mom until last year in 2016. I held it in until it destroyed me. It turned my life upside down.

Now I sit here, October 2017 an inmate in the Kent County Correctional Facility, writing a piece of my life that ended me up where I am today.

I can only think of how that damaged 3-year-old little girl still lives inside of me today. How I have ruined relationships, How I have never really loved myself. How I had completely given up on life.

Story #24: Mandi

I will never forget that November day, it had been eight long months my little Isabella fighting for her life. She had a rare form of Leukemia and we spent most of those 8 months in Helen Devos. It hurt me so much watching my daughter suffer so much and in that time I grew very angry with God and losing my faith. The pastor of our church visited every day and I started to excuse myself. I didn't want to hear what he had to say.

November 23, 2016 as I was holding Isabella she said " mommy don't hate God" an hour later at the age of 6 she passed away. Her last words to me changed my life forever. During her pain and sorrow she was selfless wanting my relationship with God to be mended. I miss my daughter more than anything in this world. Her faith to the very end taught me a lifelong lesson; death here on earth isn't final when you have Jesus as your savior. I was reminded Gog has a plan for us. My relationship with God is stronger than ever and if I never had to face this storm I can't guarantee my relationship with God would be the same but now I can cling to his promises I will see Isabella once again in Heaven.

Story #25: Haleigh

My name is Haleigh, born May 11th, 1994. Last year I went through a struggle that forever changed me as a person and made me question my faith in God. April 27th, 2016 I found out I was pregnant. My baby dad and I found out I was pregnant. My baby dad and I were filled with happiness. 3 weeks later we went to the doctors and found out we were expecting twins. The happiest day of my life turned to the worst 9 months I have ever had. I got through my first trimester of my pregnancy and got kicked out of where I was staying because my baby daddy was sneaking into my bedroom and my roommate's mother didn't like that. I was devastated. What was I going to do? How could I be so worthless I let myself lose my only place to stay. Let my baby dad tell it I was the most worthless piece of shit to walk the earth. How was I going to take care of my family? I was worthless. All I saw when I looked at myself was a worthless piece of shit. I hopped from hotel to hotel after this. Working my ass off to pay for my baby dad and I to have a place to stay.

He would start picking fights with me after a while. He called me a whore, told me his kids weren't his (but they looked just like him), I was a slut, whore, liar, fat, piece of shit, and worthless. The mental abuse turned into physical abuse. He would hit me, slam me against walls. My back teeth are missing because of him. I started to flinch when guys raised their hands next to me. 8 months pregnant I found out my baby dad had another woman pregnant due 4 months after me. He had been fucking and talking to multiple women for a while and coming home to me at night telling me he loved me. The night I found out all the dirt he had done my heart broke in my chest, it felt like the wind had been knocked out of me. All my blood drained from my face as I fell to my knees. I couldn't breathe and tears were flowing from my eyes uncontrollably. The man I loved betrayed me. The man I did everything for and taken care of took my heart from my chest and crumbled it in his hands. Until I had no love left. I truly was worthless. I felt like I wasn't a woman. I couldn't please, love, or take care of my man enough to make him love me, like I loved him. I didn't trust no man; I couldn't find myself loving anyone. His seeds I was carrying became a reminder of him every day. I almost started to resent them. Not even giving him his 1st born songs could make him love me and stay. To be faithful to me. I couldn't trust anyone, and he did that. I had no love for anyone or anything. He did that. I felt worthless, I felt like a piece of shit, I felt like dirt. He did that. I let him beat me and call me names because I thought that was one of his ways for him to show me he loved me.

I couldn't be around a man who raised his voice or a hand without me flinching. He did that. I lost faith in myself as a woman. He did that. Because of him I degraded myself. I cried myself to sleep every night. Prayed to God to make the hurt go away. Asked him every night what did I do? For him to treat me how I did. How did I fail. Because of Kwyntee, I trust a little less, I can't love fully or love how people want me to love them. I used to cry myself to sleep holding my babies. Praying they didn't look at me the way their father did. Even though he made me suffer for , forever it felt like. He gave me my wonderful Fiancé. God didn't promise happiness without pain. I never thought I could be happy again. Even though a little piece of my soul will still be missing. I will forever need to smoke my pain away, to be on anti- anxiety meds, I will always be cautious with my love and trust. All because a man didn't know how to be a MAN.

Story #26: Karla

My name is Karla. This grandma has been through a lot in her lifetime. I met my first husband when I was only 15. He was 5 years older, and I was much too young and naive to see what a con artist he was. Over time he was able to get me to think I wasn't worthy, pretty, smart, and I was lucky he wanted me. He made sure I had no friends and isolated me, all while I was just thinking I was just busy working 2 jobs to support us and taking care of the kids.

The emotional and physical abuse was tolerated until one day he decided to go off on my 11yr old daughter. When he took her down and was beating her on the ground, I knew I had to get us out. I packed her and I up and left right away. We lived in a one room efficiency apartment. My husband stalked us, threatened us, tried every intimidation method he could to get us back under his control. I had a restraining order on him during the divorce that he constantly walked through. Her changed his game and started trashing me to family, friends, church, the entire community. He used to practice in mirrors what he would say and react to scenarios. He had the church and older kids convinced I was an alcoholic even though I didn't drink, and an adulteress so I would get excommunicated from the church. The one place he never went to until he found he could con wealthy people out of money at weekly bible study.

I took care of my mom in my home for 25 years along with my kids. He decided to jump into bed with a selfish self-centered sister who loves to lie and destroy people and made up a story that I wasn't spending mom's money on her. She used her position at the sheriff department to get me charged and arrested for elder abuse. After never encountering the law before I hired a attorney. I figured all would be ok, but the judge believed her vicious story in her statement and gave me a year in jail. I now have to rebuild my life as a felon, find a job, car ,home but I will survive because I have God. With God anything is possible. He put me here for a reason. I’m sure I will be blessed when I get out and be able to show my ex and ex family that evil does not win.

Story #27: Colors

As I got older, I started learning how to love with my heart and not my eyes. I grew up hearing every insult about black and gay people. The racial and hate slurs came out of my dad's mouth. I remember it starting when I was about 15 years old. My favorite music was hip hop and rap. I loved Tupac and Lil Wayne, I had a cd player in my room and listened to it often. My dad used to come in my room and tell me to turn down that "nigger music." I was young and didn't know any better, so I just did what he asked me to do. 'He's my dad, he knows what's best for me' is what I thought to myself. As I got older and started making new friends, I found myself hanging out with people that liked " nigger music" as my dad referred to rap. My dad would talk down on my black friends and tell me how they are bad people and into drugs. Although he continued to say inappropriate comments about the things I liked and did, I was disrespecting him. I had tried to talk to my mom about my feelings because of how my dad was treating me. She had told me that my dad didn't like black people and that I should stay away from them because I'll piss him off. The only person I could turn to was my sisters and they never judged me because they were also frowned upon by our dad. Not because of who they were with but because of the choices they made. In his eyes we weren't allowed to make mistakes and that being perfect was possible. It was possible if we did what he said. When I was 20 years old, I reconnected with this guy who used to sit next to me in 10th grade. He became very interested in me and pursued me until I became his girlfriend.

My parents aren't happy for me, especially my dad. As we started dating I became distant with my parents and started spending all of my free time with my boyfriend. Whenever I was gone from home my mom would send me texts asking when I'll be coming home or why I would be gone all day. My parents interfered with my relationship. They were not supportive. Whenever I was home my dad would make crazy remarks at the dinner table without being direct. He would say black people just cheat, abuse, and take money from women. He tried to say things in hope that I would change my mind about my boyfriend, but my heart was already stuck on him.

I fell in love with him, and he always supported me and never made me feel wrong about my feelings. My dad broke my heart when he told me that if I wanted to continue dating him that I had to move out. It hurt that he didn't care about my happiness and that he was so quick to throw me out. When I had to tell my boyfriend the news they gave me, he told me I could live with him. My heart and mind were aching because I believed they would love me unconditionally like most parents did. I was only with my boyfriend for about 4 months. When I had moved out the next morning they didn't speak to me or wake up to say goodbye. When I moved my things into my boyfriend's place, I laid in bed and broke into tears. I will never forget my first true heart break. I will teach my children to love with their hearts and not their eyes.

Story #28: Kimberly

Hi, my name is Kimberly. And I'm actually going to tell you about something that I never like to talk about let alone complete strangers. When I met the author of this book you are reading now, she said she was writing a book about first heartbreak. As I got to thinking it wasn't my boyfriend, or someone I had a crush on and didn't like me back, it was my own flesh and blood my dad, Bill Heavener. You broke my heart. You started from the moment I could remember and never really stopped my first memory of you taking just a piece of my heart out is the day you made up my mom's mind to leave you I was too young to be aware that you were cheating on her, and that's not what hurt. What hurt is when it was finally quiet and I came out of my room and you were gone , and my mom was in the shower with drops of blood everywhere. Not your blood, hers. That's where it began.

I remember not seeing you much and when it was time for my bro and I to come to come to your house. There was a women I knew nothing about, along with four other kids in the house who had the upper hand and me, my brother, ½ sister, and other ½ brother who I will never claim. We were left in the dark. 2nd time you took another piece of my heart, we would come over and not see you until Sunday mornings because you and this new women were partying the whole time. So you weren't aware that the half-brother I won't claim was molesting me. I got so used to it, it was almost normal. The next part of my heart I didn't realize hurt so much was when my mom got (my bro) Keith and I dressed up all nice and said it was your special day and you should be here soon. 1,2,3 hours went by and you didn’t show. I couldn't figure out why mom took us out to eat and rent movies so late like we were getting a special treat.

The next weekend we came over and watched your wedding on a video, the woman you married was also the woman you were also cheating on my mother with. All I could think was, why wouldn't he want us there? Why is it that Keith and I look disappointed because everyone around us was in this video, laughing and having a good time and him and I are just… there. Not because we were wanted, because we had to be.

Throughout the years crumbs were just falling like when you bite into a cookie, but the cookie was my heart. All of the lies, saying you would show up for our games but wouldn't forget to pick us up for your weekends. And when we were there, we literally had to walk on eggshells. I could tell so many more stories. Being in 2nd grade telling me you were going to have my "pussy" bedsheets on the school flagpole for everyone to see. Giving my stepsister cards when she felt down and telling me toughen up. But these next two things were my final straw for the cookie to be complete crumbs.

Since I was 13, I have been in and out of the hospital for suicidal attempts. The first time I was in there as a patient at 14, they did a drug test and found methamphetamines (crystal meth) in my system. That brother that molested me for 3 years also introduced me to a new escape method, well, that's when I finally let everything out. My mom and stepdad had expected some form of sexual abuse with my sexual past. Since they found out I lost my virginity at the age of 13. I went to my dad's house when I was released from the hospital, he yelled at me. His exact words, "Do you want me to go to prison for the rest of my life?" I responded, "No." He said, "Then knock it off with the bullshit." Absolutely nothing about the meth, nothing about anything. To make it all worse, he wouldn't contact me for about a month, after all of my useless attempts, he finally messaged me via Facebook, I wasn't even worthy of a call. He asked me, "What do you want? You're Not my problem anymore!" And that's when I didn't have even close to a heart. It was broken, gone. I didn't know how to feel. All of my theories of him wanting nothing to do with me came true. Except I was a problem, to be exact, I was a drunken bowling night mistake.

So although he broke me completely, this is also about how I overcome this heartbreak. I overcame it by realizing all the good I had without him. When he isn't here to bring me down, everything around me brightens up. I came to learn that my stepfather made me realize what it was like to have an actual loving father. I am just as lucky to have that as a lot of children don't. He may have broken me, but damn he made 10x stronger. The final thing that I want to make very clear, is sometimes it is easier to let the one you love go. Because the pain you feel when consistently fighting for them is constant. But the pain you feel when you make the decision to let them go, is only for a little while. Thank you.

Story #29: Maribel

The major events in my life that mark me so I could learn how to appreciate and value life. I was 14 when my life was marked by one of the most valuable, person in my life and he decide to rape me and tell me to forget it like it never happened. My mom never believed me and when she found out our relationship broke. At the age of 17 I had an abortion that til this day I can't forgive myself for it. But at 18 I met the love of my life, (I thought). He was not handsome or cute or had a job but he had something that I love and it was that he was the leader of a gang. So we date and even thou I didn't like to many stuff that he was doing. It was to late for me to back out. At age 21, I had a son and even tho I wanted to leave him and try but I couldn't I was too scared. After going thru so much with him and his gang drive byes, fights, guns, drugs, hoes, and having 3 kids by him I decided to leave him when I caught him fucking another bitch in my house in my room in my bed. It was like all my blood went to my feet. Our house was under his moms name so I had to get out with my 3 kids and 3 trash bags full of clothes that's all I took. My world came down and my pain was so deep that it feel like I couldn't breath. I still wanted him after what he had done and the beaten he gave me that day and even with my purple blue and colorful face that I had for 2 weeks I still wanted him. But I decide to leave the state of MI and never came back. Lost everything and I started from zero. Raise my 3 kids by myself and proud to be a single mom. The lord had a teach me a lot and thank to him I'm still up and will keep on going.

There a lot I can say but I will need a notebook for it. Excuse my misspelled words ok.

Story #30: Key

I had a friend who was like my brother. We grew up together he called my mom. In 2012 he was on the run. He moved to Arizona with our mutual friend. Things didn't work so he moved to Detroit with his mom. Things didn't work there so he asked if he could move in with me. At the time I was living with mom, so I asked her. She said yes. He came to Grand Rapids came to my house we caught up cause it's been a couple months since we seen each other. I was so happy he was moving with me he inboxed and called a few girls cause he wanted to chill with some females. One told us to come over I was babysitting so I couldn't go.

He called a ride they said they a be there in 15 mins. We played 2k and took a couple of shots till his ride pulled up before he left he told me he loved me and don't fall asleep cause he was coming back. So I stayed up all night on the phone till about 5am. I fell asleep; woke up to a million phone calls saying my brother was found dead on a back porch from a bullet to his head and 6 to his body.

I froze up I wouldn't believe it my cousin took me to the hospital and his mom took me into his room to see his body. I instantly blamed myself because in the back of my mind I wanted him to stay home. With me but I let him leave. If I would have told him I wanted him to stay, he a still be here. I still cry about it my head messed up and I got trust issues because of my boy death. I'll never trust a soul.

Story #31: My First Love

I was young and very promiscuous because I was so promiscuous two brothers thought it would be a good idea to show me how to get money for sexual acts. So I stood on A street corner for about 25 minutes. I really wasn't sure what to do or what to say. I did know I didn't want to go far. I wanted to stay in eye contact of the two brothers, so the guy just parked at the end of the street. I was with him about 5 minutes and made $60. I gave each brother $20 and told them thank you and told them to go on their way and they did. I started running away from home and found myself sleeping in a crack house and standing on the street corner for hours on out for chump change.

At this crack house I met a man. He was a crack dealer. It was love at first sight I thought. He would take me with him periodically. This would really make me happy. I was always so full of joy when I was with him. His joy was money I got to realize that real fast. So I eventually would go stand on the street corner more often to get money to be with him more often. When in all reality he really wasn't spending any more or any less time with me. Then the truth was finally came out. He was in love with someone already. He even had a kid on the way. I was literally 14 years old at the time and I was broken.

Story #32: Tammy

I'm Tammy. I grew up in a dysfunctional family. Mom and dad were divorced since I was 3. Mom had a lot of different men. I was exposed to abuse, emotionally, sexually, and physically, I saw my dad on visitations in my childhood. He was good to me. He was a Hippie., He had long hair, he smoked weed and sold it. I was around rooms and cars so filled with smoke I could not see. I grew up an addict and always had lots of boyfriends sometimes I was not only a 2 timer, but I was also a 10 timer. I was married once.

All my men were addicts. I started out at 13 with weed. At 16 I moved in with a man who was 29, he sold weed. We must have smoked 10 joints a day. I was with him for 9 years. His name was Dick. We fought a lot. He pushed me around, held me down, chased me, tackled me, Never hit me. Our last fight I threw a glass platter on the floor, and he picked up a sharp piece of the platter and threatened me with it. He also was good at flipping the bed upside down. While I'm in it Ignoring him. When he left to go to work I was crying. I felt unloved, unwanted, I was angry. I wanted to leave him. We had a child together. Dixon was then 3 years old. I called a shelter- every woman's place In Muskegon. I was crying telling them of our fight. They told me to come stay at the shelter and that they could help me get food and rent assistance for my own apartment. And that is what I did. I had a police officer take me to meet a lady from the shelter at McDonald's.)

After having my own apartment I was lonely. I stared out the window wishing Dick my sons' father would come to see us. But he didn't. I was sad and depressed of the 9 years I was with him, he had strong control over me. I never had a job. Never saw my family. I was mad at my mom for how I was raised. When Dixon was 4 my mom called me to patch up what happened we had a nice birthday party for Dixon. She was a better Grama then a mom.

Story #33: Dana

My name is Dana. I was born November 6, 1976. The first time I ever had felt an emotional pain I couldn't get over was when I met a guy named Matt. We met Aug 2006 everything was amazing in the beginning just as I wanted it to be and pictured a perfect life with him until later on in our relationship I found out that he was an alcoholic a very bad one and then everything had falling apart. He had become verbal and physical towards me emotionally abusive. In those situations it made me feel weak, terrible, worthless, downgraded. Matt called me a whore because I had looked in the mirror and asked myself if I am a whore… after that I cried my eyes out for days my eyes where puffy and swollen. I never had anyone ever talk that way to me before from that situation I lost self-worth it took me a long time to build the women I am today. I think if Matt could have stayed sober our relationship would of been beneficial to both of us. I feel that in that time of my life was a turning point if he wasn't emotionally abusive I wouldn't be ok with disrespecting my children's fathers and emotionally abusing them treating my kid's fathers like shit I feel that Karma came back to me.

Story #34: Sorry

The choices we make,
The laws that we break,
The hurt that I caused
For going A- Wall:
I am truly sorry…
Trying to hold it together,
Knowing this story isn't forever'
I wanna hug my kids,
And just 4 get what I did:
I truly am sorry…
Everything happens for a reason,
In 2 months I'll be leaving,
Leaving this life way behind me,
For I am a woman who is free:
I truly am sorry…
I'm changing my life around,
Never wearing a frown,
God is good and helped me thru this,
But I never will forget what I did:
I truly am sorry…
I'm ending this with a goodbye and God bless,
When I get out,
That will be the test,

To make choices that are right,
With The Almighty God by my side:
Thank you Jesus

Story #35 "Wishing You the Best"

Giving you my all,

We all know at these point in times we're all able to fall…

Just Look at how far you have come,

Promise you will not be done…

We are all here to make sure you're not alone,

To make sure you never forget home,

We want to see you do your time and graduate,

Without a hesitate…

You have made it so far on your journey,

Always keep in mind you are very worthy..

We are here for you to listen comfort and hug,

Just think growing up this is your only drug,

Please keep in mind on the things that needs to be done,

Son I will be done hun…

Hope you keep your sane,

Soon no longer pain..

"Wishing you the best"

Story #36: Heartbreak

Let me see… where do I start. It seems to me that this life of mine has been full of heartbreak. From growing up with a mom with hepatitis C. which back then was a terminal illness. And having to visit her in a hospital bed, scared that every time I left the hospital that it was going to be the last time I would see her. Then having to go to school and put a smile on my face like nothing was wrong. That's why I never miss the chance to tell the people I care about that I love them. Because I know that life is a fragile thing and nothing last forever.

I remember I was acting a fool when I was like 12-13. I just got out of juvenile, and she sat me down and read her letters to me that she wrote for me and my bro when the doctors told her she was going to die. That was one of the hardest things to heat still to this day. What do you do with that shit? I was actually mad at her for doing that. I never thought about it till now, but her being here still is a miracle.

Another heart-breaking situation was finding my bro dead. That was my right-hand man. I would've taken a bullet for him. I actually took a drug charge for him. He taught me a lot some good and some bad. We've been to war together. When he got paralyzed everyone left all his friends his girls. I didn't tho that shit made us closer. I used to take him with me everywhere, It was almost like the roles were reversed, I was the Big bro now. We'd go out I used to make the hoes dance on him, at the strip club. He used to love that shit; we'd have so much fun that was my big bro… But every time we would get back to the crib, and I would pick him up out of his chair to put him in his bed. He would always tell me he was sorry, as if he was a burden to me or something. That would fuck me up because we was just having fun I guess. Reality would kick in that he was paralyzed from the neck down. He would tell me he wanted to die. I'd tell him stop playing, but I could see in his eyes he was serious, and he had given up. I sat and watched him die a lil bit every day. Then one day I went in to get out of bed to start his day, I stood by his bed and seen wasn't breathing. I looked at his face he was gone he was so cold. I know he had to of been dead for hours. I know there was nothing that could be done. Me and my sis Jen tried CPR. The medics came and said the same thing there's nothing left.

After everyone left we was waiting for the people to come get his body. I sat in the room with him alone and talked to him for about an hour. I said I bet your punk ass is up there dancing right now and I'm down here all sad and shit. I waited until the people got there put my hand on the top of his head told him I loved him, and I'd miss him and that was that.

Then my pops killed himself that was rough. That happen not even six months after my bro died. I remember the day it happened. I talked to him earlier. I asked what he was up to? He told me Joe I'm just tired my dad was addicted to pills at this time in my life. He asked if I wanted him to get off of them. I still think if I would have just gave him some he would still be here I don't know.

Any ways I was beefing with my bm at the time, so I was staying at my Grandmother's crib she was in AZ at the time, so her house was empty. I get a call from my mom she was crying. I asked her what was wrong? She said your dad is dead. I told her that can't be I just talked to him. SO I hung up called my stepmother. I asked her what happen? Sher said she went downstairs, and she found him down there, she said the barrel of the shot gun was still in his mouth and the top of his head was gone. That put me in a real bad place, and I didn't get better until I met my wife. Another heartbreaking situation. Was coming to prison. Getting all this time and watching everybody change up on me. Its heartbreaking to sit in here and watch everyone move on. Not that they shouldn't because it no one's fault but my own for being in here. But you can't help to think that's supposed to be my life that someone else is living with my wife. Or that's supposed to be my child… Heartbreak is when you have 5 kids you consider to be your kin and you only get to see 1 of them. Or when you 150 miles away, but you might as well be on the other side of the world because ain't one coming. Heartbreak is when you love someone so much that when you see her cry you cry. Heartbreak is when you know what would've been but this prison shit made it so it can't be anymore. Heartbreak is when your grasping on to the last few threads of your perfect life you had before this prison shit happened, because you are scared of the heartbreak of losing the love of your life. Heartbreak is having to let go of the person that made you the happiest. Yea… I know a lot about heartbreak.

Below are the original workings of the writers involved in putting this together. Special thanks to the talented women from the KCCF.

11/06/2017

"Looking at you daily"

Looking at your faces day to day.
Wishing I could take this pain away . . .
Memories of you going through my mind,
It never stops it feels like its constant rewind. . .
Every night before I close my eyes,
I think about all my white lies . . .
I am so sorry another time in here,
Im very thankful just not another year . .
Nightly I stare at you guys,
Wishing this was just another dream in disguise .
Hoping to wake up next to you,
And be done playing this charades game too .
After this is all over,
I will never forget the words Rover . .
I am so ready for the day,
I can again see you face to face,
And never again want my own space .
Looking at your faces day to day,
Soon this pain will be far away [redacted]

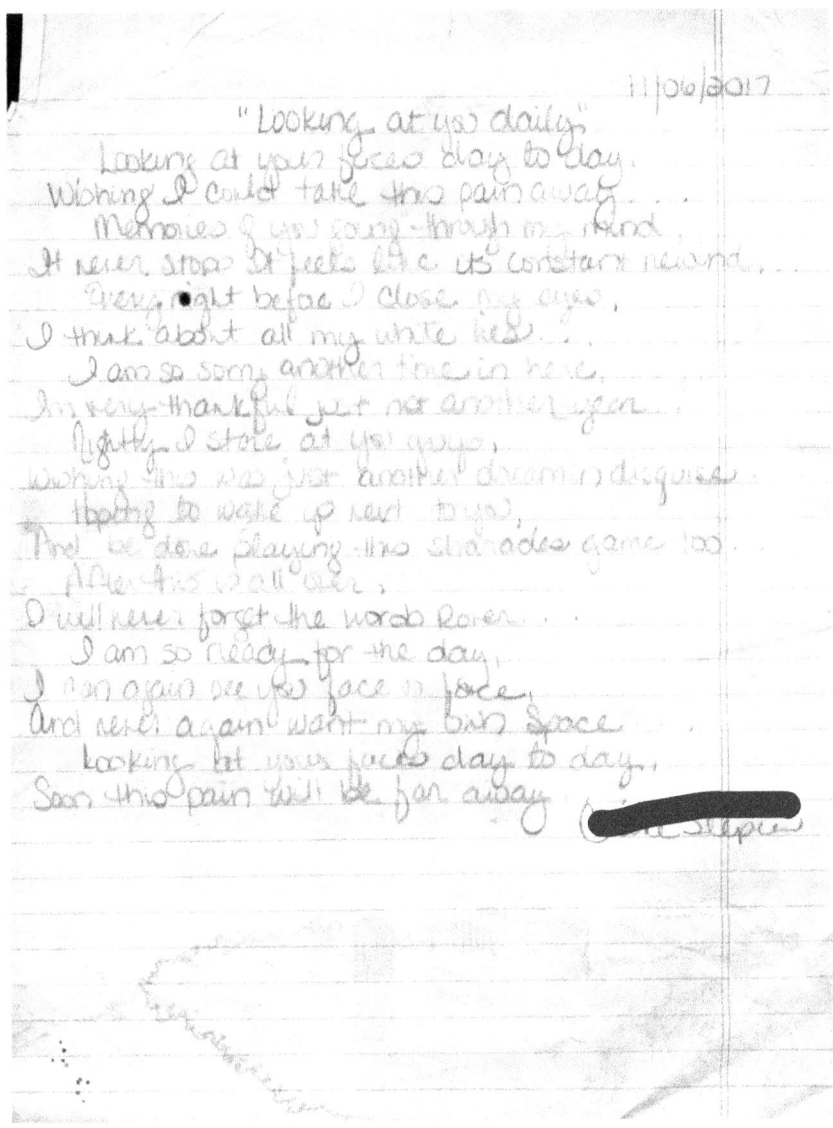

- 2008

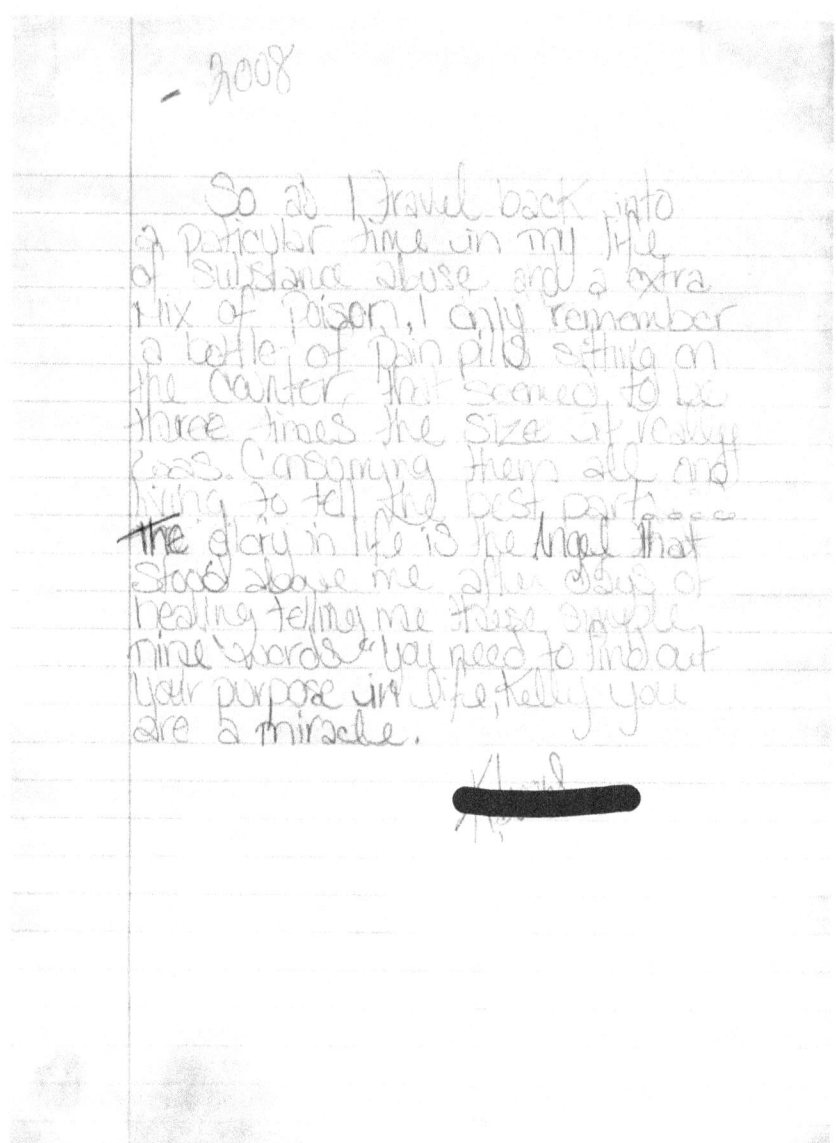

So as I travel back into a particular time in my life of substance abuse and a extra mix of poison, I only remember a bottle of pain pills sitting on the counter that seemed to be three times the size it really was. Consuming them all and living to tell the best part... The glory in life is the Angel that stood above me after days of healing telling me these simple nine words "you need to find out your purpose in life, Kelly you are a miracle.

[redacted]

11/06/2017

"Our family"

We are never weak.
We are very strong.
We are never wrong.
But are family grows forever long,
And forever us belong

We as a family will always seek the path,
we will always live daily in our wrath
We will never forget where are love comes from
Never abuse nor some
We are a family that comes in different kin
You will never know, what is going thru our mind

But no matter where we go,
Us family will always be joined toe to toe
We are never weak,
We are very strong.
"Are family sticks forever long!"

[illegible]

11/13/2017

"Strong Enough"

Those that don't know me, I am a fighter
and will fight until its over.
B3 no class or me, Still mini deputy. . .
I tried, I tried to stick, stay, may
have to now go away. .
Not for long.
But they did play me wrong.
like a war.
I did put it apon you kids with a
sword.
Not good enough,
Those bitches all just thought they were
tough. .
This time I have tried,
And yet havent lied
All these ppl know me,
Their just hating you see . . .
So like I said if I end up in the hole,
Just remember I tried playing my role . . .
Only you kids know,
You know Im not out like no hoe
I hope you all realise,
With my experience you'll think wise.
Know all bitches are fake,
They all are snakes.
Maybe one day they'll all awake.
I will die trying.
Never lying . . .

Strong Enough
Cherie St

Br [redacted]

Well I can say it all started by the age of 12. I started looking for love in all the wrong places and I guess you can say "I found it"! I am the baby of six girls and I grew up in a fatherless home. I always thought I was wise beyond my years, so I thought I could handle what "Big Girl" territory brought. I became pregnant at the age of 12 and gave birth at 13. My so called first "Love", who was the same age as me, denied me and his first born son. I guess it was all good when I gave up the goods, but when the going got tough, he kept it moving! My heart was torn into pieces, only behind close doors because I wanted to keep up this imaage that no one or nothing could hurt me! So the year of [redacted] I entered High School, Brandon was 1 years old and I thought I had it all together!! My mind was in my books and I felt in charge of my heart again. Febuary of "98" comes and I met the most handsome, charming young man ever! This (gentlement) swept me off my feet! He knew what to say and just how to say it! All along he was a monster in disguise! He beat me for 11 years from the time I was 14 until I was 25 years old. I bore 5 of his children and buried one as well due to the domestic volience I went in labor early with he and I daughter Shania Lynn Allen (our 3rd child). But there is always light at the end of the tunnel, God rescued me and showed me his love is all the love I need! Through Christ I learned to love myself and others with the love of God and also that I am a Conqueror not a victim anymore!!

(1)

"I don't know how to tell you kids this, but you're mother just expired," my grandfather's baritone voice let out as he walked across the dining room in his and my grandmother's city flat. He hung up the phone just moments earlier with the hospital. I sunk into the old, large sofa and looked across the room to my small brother sitting on the other couch. His face turned bright red, he held his breath, and tears started drenching his chubby cheeks. That was my cue to play big sister. I leapt up off the couch and embraced him with my whole upper body. "It will be OK. I promise it will be OK. Don't be sad. We will be OK." His tears drenched my shoulder. I didn't cry. He was a month from turning 13, and I was 14.

My mothers death was the most tragic thing I've ever experienced. Throughout most of my young life with her - we fought. There was little love expressed between the two of us. Aside from a handful of random memories when I was too small to really notice, most of my memories of her are filled with anger, tears, resentment, and a very sad woman. She rarely smiled, except when she was with a few select friends getting high. She hated my father. She would cheat on him regularly and would bring me, my brother, and my sister as accomplices. Often we were left alone in some strangers living room while she escaped behind closed doors to emerge with a laugh and smile. I could never make her smile the way her special "private" friends and drugs could. I would do everything she asked me to, and it was never enough. I could "always do better" she would say. And deep down, I knew I could too.

Sometimes she would cry alone in her room, for hours on end. I would sheepishly knock on her bedroom door and ask what was wrong. She'd tell me to go away, or even be so honest to tell me she wanted to die and wanted to kill herself. I didn't understand why we weren't enough for her to live for or make her happy. So I would keep trying.

As we got older, my sister became more rebellious. She was always getting reprimanded at school. My mom and her developed a very tight bond, and would do a lot of things together privately. My sister began to torment me - and my mother would always defend her. She always blamed it on my sister being mixed race and I had it easy because I was white with blonde hair and blue eyes.

Over time I learned to stay closer to my dad. Despite his tumultuous and abusive relationship with my mother, he was a loyal and tender father. He tried to spoil me, because he didn't disagree with my cries that my mother didn't love me. We'd go for long drives and listen to music, or take trips into the city to my grandmother's house where I'd cry over my mother being so mean and hurtful, her wicked physical abuse, and her cold and unloving nature. My grandmother would hug me and share that her mother didn't love her either. "If only I could do better," I kept thinking. No matter how much my dad loved and spoiled me, and my grandmother related to me, I craved my mother's love and recognition more than anything.

(2)

Middle school approached and hormones set in. My sister became more and more rebellious, my brother immersed himself in sports, and my father fell further and further into his depression. He had gone in and out of rehabs, making promises to my mother and breaking them, and she continued cheating, lying, and crying. She was always high. I learned to hide in my bedroom when she was home, and time my day according to her schedule to avoid her. If I ever crossed her path I said few words, and she would snicker and make degrading comments. But I still did all I could. I received straight A's in school, won all awards, was captain of all my sports teams, and was the president of as many clubs as I could sign up for. My bedroom wall was covered with certificates. None of it mattered. I didn't exist. And when I did, I was her verbal and physical punching bag.

I would journal nightly my rage and hurt over my mom and my sister. They ganged up on me and I never could understand why I couldn't earn her love despite all my work on being her perfect child. My sister, the trouble-maker and rebel, got all the attention and forgiveness. I was a shadow. And I was angry, sad and lonely.

One day, sitting on the toilet, my mother called me in and told me she understood why I hated her. I told her I didn't. She said she knew I did, and didn't blame me, because she hated her mother too. I trembled when she talked to me, never knowing if what I said would be right or wrong, and

I wanted to yell to her "Why don't you love me? I'm a kid! I don't hate you I want to love you." But I couldn't. She told me that she thought her and I were a lot alike, and that is why we didn't like each other. She said that when I got older, I'd understand her better, and we might get along better. So that is what I did, I decided to focus on the future, forget about my childhood, and obsess about being an adult with an adult life, so then, finally, I could have my mother, and her acceptance, approval, and love for me. We could have what her and my sister had, but better.

I decided I wanted to be an archutect so I could build and design her ideal house. We were poor and lived in a trailer. My mom always complained and cried about not having enough money. That we shouldn't live in a trailer. So I'd make a bunch of money, give it to her and buy her whatever she wanted, and design and build her dream house. I sketched all the time. I fantisized about big, fancy colleges, and being successful. I wouldn't be what her and my dad were. Not ever.

When she suddenly died in the winter of my freshman year of high school, my heart broke into a million tiny peices. Shattered. I stared blankly at the TV screen as they played my mom's story over and over again on the news. "Tragedy," they all called it. Was it? Was it an accident. She was high and walked out into the middle of the semi frozen lake and fell through? She spoke of death constantly. Was she

(3)

finally free? Free of her suffering, free of being my mom?

As I walked into the waiting room of the hospital, a large group of people looked up and stared at us, holding their breath, all I could mutter was "I need to see my mom." "Honey, you can't," my aunt said. "I have to. I need to talk to her." "But she's not in good shape." She was already dead. She died before they pulled her in from the frozen lake. I looked firmly back at my aunt. "I need to see her. I have to tell her something!" Her eyes filled up, she walked across the room to the nurse, and then motioned me over.

They walked my brother and I into the sterile room, my aunt holding my hand, my dad holding my brother's. My uncle, already in the room, crying. Tubes came out of multiple parts of her body, and she covered the entire bed. She was a larger woman, but water had filled her body so much, she was swollen and unrecognizable. I'll never forget that image. I laid myself across her stomach with my arms stretched out across her and all I could repeat was "I'm so sorry. I'm so sorry for everything. I'm so sorry I wasn't enough. I'm so sorry we didn't get along. I'm so sorry I didn't make your dreams come true." I began to wail. The room filled up with tears and that's when my aunt grabbed me and said it was time to go. I told her I wasn't done yet. She said she knew, but the doctors needed the room.

Just like that, my plan was over. I'd never be able to win her love and attention. I never got the chance. I never got the chance to get those warm hugs, gentle kisses, the "its ok," the pats on the back, the security of knowing I was OK an accepted. That I was enough.

Everyday since, I've struggled with alcohol addiction, infidelity, toxic friendships and relationships, issues with money, self worth, and my identity. My youth was spent trying to prove myself and win my mother's love, and becoming something I thought she wanted. When she died, although she was gone in the physical sense, the programming within me remained. I spent all of my high school years, college, and well into my 30's trying to prove myself and be something worthy of love. But it was never enough. I hated myself. I hated the person I was obsessed at becoming, and I hated that I couldn't even be perfect enough at mastering this shell and facade I wanted so badly to be.

As I slowly began to embrace the breakdown, the unraveling, the imperfections, and the beauty in the mess, the self-acceptance takes place. The beauty and the love is in the mess, not the unattainable perfections. I don't know what my mom would think of me today. I don't know if we'd be friends. I don't know if she'd be proud of me or not. Its one of the mysteries I'll have to live with forever. But in the meantime, I'm learning to love & be friends with myself.

Well Starting today was about the biggest slap in the Face ever I had got news From my loving sister that my aunt that I love So much had passed away while I have been in here incarcerated For about 4 months Now I have been waiting For these people to give me any news that [illegible] I will be going through Drug Court soon, the guy had told me that he will be seeing me Monday which is Monday now and no word from him yet. It's Crazy because I am here and it's like 6:30pm and nothing yet. and I am So stressed out, I'm Lost, Lonely, Worried, Scared, Sad, angry and not able to do anything. like my hands are tied behind my back and Someone just Keeps punching me in my Stomache. I [illegible] to argue with my ex husband again

Just to put something in
my account. when the bastard
owes me everything in this world
it's pathetic he can manipulate
me and abuse me. and "able
to get away with it and still
able to talk to me with Disrespect
and able to even raise his voice
to me. but on top of all that
still not able to even pray over
my aunt. She was the sweetest
person ever She told it how
it was and didn't care if She
told the truth as long as it
was the truth. She cared For
others so much and she
had so much love and her
poor cats will miss her dearly.
She loved them so much.
If I was there I would
be able to Fix some of the
things that She needed to be
Fixed. Thank GOD. that I
still have Faith in him and
that will never Stop.

I just hope the best for tomorrow and believe I will be able to Stay Strong. I am Sober and that is the best thing that I have now and my relationship with GOD, it's such a blessing but I will miss my Aunt Dearly. and I pray that they don't hurt her cats because that's what She loved so Dearly. I have Faith that I will hear Soon but now that my Aunt is Gone, I'm So lost and alone but not really. I know GOD is beside me each and everyday but it wont be the Same anymore I Still plan to Stay Sober and focused to Stay Strong and I believe that things will be better or if they are getting worst it doesn't mean I will loose my Faith.

I will Stay Sober and Focused and it is going to be a little bit of a Challange, but I have Faith in everyday, and I plan not to Worry about tomorrow but let tomorrow worry For itself. Well I hope one day I will be able to be an inspiration to Someone that needs a Shoulder. I need to appreciate life and apreciate every breath I Still have in my body; But I will keep my head up and move through with all that GOD has For me. thank you For hearing my Story For what it is and I have learned from it too. I just need a Shoulder or an act that Someone Cares at this moment.

I have had many heartbreaks throughout my life. My first, hardest heartbreak happen when I was #23 years old and lasted as long as #7 plus years, until I was almost #31 years old. During that period of time I went through a lot of changes mentally and physically. It was like "pain is love." Which in the end I believe made me a better, stronger, spiritual and conscience person. But first was my actions. At #23 years old I had everything I could ever wanted. House, new car, my girl our son, money, clothes, and travel to different places whenever I wanted. I loved the life I lived, and the heart of it was spent in the streets to provide for this life style. Thinking I was making my family happy when I should have just been there doing the right things to provide for our needs. But they never knew all the chances I was taking for my money. I was young, naive and only thinking of myself

1 of 4

My thinking at #23 was to get money every hour of the day by any means possible. Not really realizing the hurt and pain that I was causing my family with my mind set. All it took was one bad night, one bad hour, from many bad decisions that led me astray. And that night was when I helped pull a armed robbery. No it wasn't my first and I wasn't hurting for money. But it was my last armed robbery that put me in prison. I have never been locked up no more than a few days and now I was facing years in prison. As I sit in that cell handcuffed all I could think of was my son and how I let him down as a father. Yes, I cried. But my tears couldn't save me. Before all of this we would spend every day together playing going on car rides visiting friends and family. Now in less then a day Dad is gone for years and years. While I was locked up and away, I would hear stories about how my son would wait at

2 of 4

the front door or stare out the window looking for his Dad to come home. In prison I would try to run from this pain by not calling anyone for long periods of time. Plus, I would workout until my muscles hurt causing pain to myself. Day after day, year after year I would chase physically pain to get away from the mental pain. It was my outlet. A way to live without love from my family. Because I felt powerless to help or do anything. When my son would come to visit me while I was in prison, it was heart breaking to see him come and go. He would tell me, "Dad I'ma get you out of here". He was so passianate in his eyes about getting me out I could not even respond. He was growing without me. I was not there to see it and give him my love for so many years. I remember sitting outside or in my room imaging that me and my son were out having fun at a park or a beach. I would find me laughing at myself some times.

3 of 4

Than a fight would breakout and someone was stabbed and then I was back to reality that I was stuck in prison where there's no love with more years to go. There where days I felt like giving up. I was gone for so long that I felt like I would never get out of that place. It was like trying to live life in a coffin. On my visit with my son I told him, "Words can not express how bad I feel for not being there with you son." Then he hit me with these words that put me back on focus when ever I felt down and out. He told me, "Dad, I'm not mad at you because I love you." Those words coming from my 5 year old son still sticks to me till this very day. I live off them words every time before I do anything that can get me years in prison.

CG

4 of 4

All my life I've been the problem
Child it never fails being in jail,
prequant at 16 not finishing School
Can't keep a job, just Not doing
anything right. Hear my story....
I had a wonderful childhood my
mom worked hours to provide for
us. Dad was in and out When I
was about 7 or 10 that age a little
blurr. He was drugged out he was
my first heartbreak but he wasn't
my last. the father of my Child
left me hurt, Confused, brusied,
burned, basically DEAD. My heart
longed for him I put him first,
Every Relationship starts off Great
just like this one, he said he loved
me, I was his one and only he
Said he waited for me I was
15yrs old he was 18yrs old. We
well I waited till was 16yrs old
to have sex with him the Day
I turned 16yrs old he asked me to
have his Child And I was inlove

with him that I gave in I wasnt
thinking about my life I wanted to
make him Happy I didnt want
him to leave me, I thought he was
going to be a great dad Never be
like mines. I said yes I'll have
your Child I told him everything
gave him all of me and soon as
he knew he had me Right where
he wanted it was DONE. I was
holding my first Child at 16 yrs old
and wasn't Due till November 15th
I found out I was prequant April
8th I was inlove so Nobody opiaun
matter but his He started being
absuvive and slapping me,
punching me I was 6 months
When he punched me in my
Chest and kicked me out of
his house bloody Nose

My name is Mindy and this is my Story. It will be a Short Version cause the long Version is just to much for you and I. Also, Im not Sure that doing this. What feelings will evolve that Im afraid of all over again. I had a great upbring. I went to Church. My family didnt fight, or drink or do drugs. They were very strict with me. A white picket fence family. I meet my husband whom is the father of my 3 sons. We were married for 13 years. I had feelings he was Cheating and doing things he shouldnt. But who wants to believe that when you think life is great and you now have your own white picket fence, or so you think.

The last straw was probably the 10th girl. (whom range in age from 18 to 51) I was pregnant with my 3rd Son, 7 months along. When I found out I was so distraught. I couldnt figure out what was wrong with me. I figured it was time to put my foot down, no more games between us, no more lies. I divorced the man I thought was the love of my life. I remember just crying all day, every day. I had already had my Son So I started drinking alot. Not remembering why I was waking up in bed next to my parents. with swollen eyes again from drinking and crying again all night. I was so disgusted in myself. I had this guilt for myself I didn't deserve. I delt with him for as long as I did and that was nothing but my fault. I needed to man up and stop crying and drinking and take care of my kids. I struggled. It was hard. I was discouraged I couldn't do better for my kids. life went on. I picked myself up off the ground more times than I can count. I eventually ran into my highschool Sweetheart. In high school he was sweet, he was "that man" but it was school we were kids, unsteady.

He and I started to date again. We went on with dating for a couple years. He moved in and we built a life together. He was great with my kids. He and my ex got along great, Co-parenting worked good.

I was excited, happy, in love; I was on top of the world. Something I said I would never ever do again... I married him. Another huge beautiful wedding. Life was perfect. Awhile into our marriage pain pills turned into drugs. Hard core drugs. Our relationship started to fuse, Not Romantically anymore but Verbally. Mental abuse, emotional abuse and then came the Physical. when there wasnt enough drugs it was my fault, I was always hidding something from him he thought.

Hes 3x's bigger than me. I was and still am very intimadated by him. I make sure to this day he has no idea where I reside. The days got longer and we got higher. I gave my kids to thier dad a lot more than was ok. I was worthless. I was getting

My ass beat daily. learning to like the taste of my own blood. going to bed at night dreaming about my own coffin colors, waking up Crying Cause my kids werent even Crying at thier own Mothers funeral. I was on my hands and knees with my heart on the grand begging and praying for my life. even tho I felt I didnt deserve any bit of it. I was willing to beg for my fake white picket fence life back. I was willing to live fake, betrayed and unloved. But its hard to leave someone you think you love so much. And really to be honest. I feel I really do love him still. I feel he was my soul mate. there are a lot of parts to this story that I left out that I just Cant write about. like when in 2014 he tried to kill me with a car. I Cant actually write it all down and do it and feel it all over again right now. Im Sorry for that.

But in the end of all this. My feelings and my feelings today are numbness. I hope that all these feelings dont leave me numb to a lot of situations forever.

By the way I am divorced now and he fought it hard, begged to change. I almost at one point reget it. Reget isnt a good feeling along with numbness. Regret and numbness = lonely. I hope I dont feel that forever.

It was a normal Spring day in 1991. My brother and I had gone to school like we always did. I was 15 and a Sophmore in high school.

We returned home around 3pm and finished our chores. I was on the corded phone we had in the kitchen on the wall, when my father returned home from work. He proceeded to his favorite lazy boy in front of the T.V. like he had for years prior to that day. I made him some food and served it to him in his chair & then proceeded to get back on the phone, as teenage girls do. My father wanted me to take care his plate, I said I would after I got off the phone. He proceeded

to get up, threw me up
against the wall.
A little while later after
my brother and father fought,
I called my mother at work
and told her what happened.
After 27 yrs of marriage,
that incident made my
mother divorce my father.
He never fully recovered
from the divorce. My
brother + I, were also, never
the same after being uprooted
half way through our
sophmore year of high
school.
I have always wondered
where we would be, or how different
my life would be, had I just
did what he asked that day.
My father never dated
anyone else, he said my Mother
was the only women he ever
loved, all the way til the
day he died.

Had I reacted differently,
would he still be here?
Would my Mother still be
alone, as she never dated
anyone else as well.
Things I will never know,
and live with everyday.

Tami

My first heart break -

I grew up fast ment my husband at the age of 17, pregant by 18 and gave birth to my baby girl at the age of 19 [redacted] - It was love at first site - married by the age of 22 - we went to vegas and got married - It was awesome had family and friends go with us - Had the time of are lives :) - me and my husband were living the good life - both had good Job's - had a wonderful little girl - bought a house - had 2 car's - went to football games and concert's all the time - had a wonderful marriage: Four year's into are marriage me and my husband decided to have one more Kid - Well we got pregant with twins - on Sept. 1 we had 2 tiny babies - 2 boy's - Life was complete - So I thought - I started to notice that my husband wasn't himself after the twins were born - He wasn't home alot - I started to notice that he was spending money that he could not explain - where he spent it - He wasn't so good

to me anymore - like he used to be -
emoinally or phacilly - one of are
friend's said that they thought he
was using hard drug's - my first thought's
were - "no way" - he would never do
that - and hide it from me - so being
the women that I am - I started
to snop on him - go thraugh his thing's
and found proof that he was - I asked
him about it - he told me the truth - that
he was - I told him he needed to get
help or leave, not going to have that
around our kids - so he choose to leave -
left me with a 7 yr old and 2
babies - well to top it all off when
he left me - He went to a girl that
he had been cheating on me with -
when I found out about her - once
again - I asked him, and he
said that he had been cheating on me
with her for awhile - in that moment -
my heart fell out of my chest - broken
into pieces - never had I ever thought
that he would do that - that was
the first time I had my heart broken.

My story is pretty simple, at least compared to others. Writing this makes me feel self-righteous and thats a feeling I do not like. However I need to keep in mind that hopefully these words help others.

To sum up what has effected me the most is easy - ME. Its all about me. It always has been. I never knew how selfish I am until I went to jail for the third time for Drunk Driving.

I was arrested off the end of a very long night. I worked my 12hr shift and went to two local bars ~~that~~ where I knew the bartenders. I was with my ex girlfriend and we were of course drunk. My ex is a full blown alcoholic so being around her is hard not to drink. Leaving the second bar at 3am, she begged me not to drive. I of course told her I can do whatever I want. I never took anyone's opinion or ~~well~~ well fare into consideration. I hurt so many people by my thoughtless actions. I was of course arrested. And in turn created a whirlwind of emotions. For the first time I realized that I was my worst enemy.

I learned to love myself thru this process, and put others above me. I do not need my old self anymore. Thinking of others first has given me all the fullfilment I need.

There was once this beautiful young mom. She was all alone in a foreign city known for making cars. She was 19 with her first brand new baby girl and they lived in a run down trailer, her very own first place as a grown Mother. It was December and all she could worry about was if her newborn daughter was warm enough w/o heat and a blizzard outside. She would layer blankets on the crib matress and line the walls of it with blankets, rape her in her crib blanket and then cover the top of the crib w/ blankets. Her baby seemed so warm and content and so amazing and beautiful. The young mom was so proud of the life she created and the changes she was making to be the best mother she could be. So many hopes, plans and dreams filled her head whenever she held her baby. So much Love.

The young mother did not have a relationship w/ her own parents since she'd left after an argument 3 years ago. However now that her baby was 1y/o she wanted her daughter to know her grandparents, and they were excited to meet their new granddaughter. To the mom's surprise, her parents rejected her baby! The grandparents were furious that her daughter was of color! The young mother was so hurt by their reaction, she cursed them and vowed to never speak to them again! "How could they be so cruel to deny my beautiful baby? Don't they see my eyes, myself in her? They must not love me either!" she thought.

2 years passed and her baby grew happy, healthy and bright as a star! The mother was in bliss whenever she looked at her baby. She worked very hard to support them both and her daughter would go to her father's house while she was working. One day when they returned home she gave her baby, now 3 years old, a bath before bed, when she noticed a stench and some discharges! She took her to her doctor the next day and they ran some test. "What could be wrong with my baby?" she thought. Maybe an allergic reaction to the soap she used.

But when the doctor came back w/ results and a few other people, she knew something was wrong. The doctor then said, "I'm sad to say that these people are from Child Protective Services. Your daughter's test came back positive for chlamydia." She was so confused! Words couldn't express her thoughts but lost for words.

Many years of therapy, court, and heartache followed, well into her baby's adult years with her grandparents right beside her, and her father. God carrying them all along the way.

Hi, I'm Lauren. Usually when girls talk about their first heart break, its about some boy who promised to give them the world, but left them with nothing. Well mine is not quite the usual heart break. My first heart break was given to me by my Mother. Daughters are supposed to feel loved, protected, happy, supported, guided, and so much more by their Mothers. But I felt none of that by mine. What I felt was abandonment, unsafe, depressed, unloved, and alone. Drugs, Money, and men are what my Mom chose to love. My brother and I grew up thinking having a Mom coming and going as she pleases and leaving us with random people was normal. Well its not. If it wasn't for my brother, I may not have even been here today. Fun family nights with Mom consisted of going to the bar, sitting and watching her have fun. Sometimes we got to play pool or some other game. But mostly we walked off and would go outside, and go on adventures. By the time my Mom even noticed my brother and I were gone, it would have been too late. One time Nick and I got bored and walked off outside. There was train tracks on the side of the bar. We decided to go walk on them and get away from all the drunk adults. We got pretty far down the tracks, and came up to a small man made lake. We started picking up small rocks and throwing them in the lake. Nick turned around and seen someone walking towards us. So he grabbed my arm, and pulled me in the bushes, and we started walking into a ditch. The man walked up, and was looking around. We knew he was looking for us. He was the same guy sitting alone in the bar. He had followed us. Nick and I sat still until he continued walking. When we couldn't see him any more we came out of the bushes, and started walking fast back to the bar. The train tracks were about twenty or so feet above the lake. So we were trying to be careful, but we heard the guy yell at us. So we started to run. I tripped and fell 20 feet down into the water. I smacked my head on something in the water, and got knocked out. My brother I guess ran down the side of the tracks and jumped into the water and grabbed me. Once my brother pulled me out of the water, the man who followed us, picked me up.

He took me back to the bar and Nick followed. I guess my Mom had sent him, instead of getting us herself. He walked in with us, and I started to wake up in my Moms lap, while she was taking care of my head wound in the bathroom. The guy ended up taking us all home. My Mom seemed more angry than worried. She asked why we wondered off, and we said because its not fun to be around drunk adults. Not much was said after that. That is just one of many bad incidents that were caused by my Mom not caring enough. But we were blessed with an amazing Dad. I'm thankful to have him. If it wasn't for my Mom, I wouldn't be who I am today. I am strong, and know what not to do as a Mother.

Friend's & Family

Friend's & Family are why we are here
Keep the one's you love near
Friend's I Love you so much
You are all part of me,
that no one can touch
Alot of what I say & do
in alot of way reflects on you
You are there for me
when no one else could be
I love you all for that
I even tip my hat
Time goes so fast
But our love is what makes it last
I hope to have you all forever
Through fights, money or whatever
we all have alot of fun
when all is said and done

[redacted]

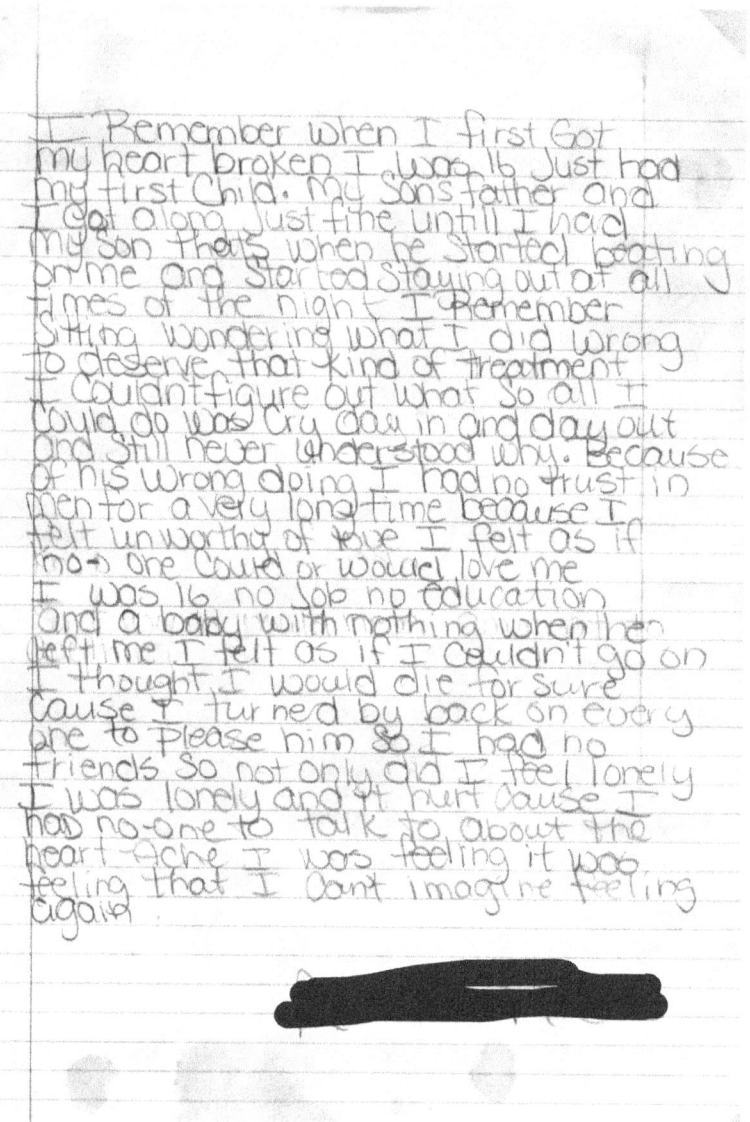

I Remember when I first Got
my heart broken I was 16 Just had
my first Child. My Sons father and
I Got along Just fine untill I had
my Son that's when he Started beating
on me and Started Staying out at all
times of the night I Remember
Sitting wondering what I did wrong
to deserve that kind of treatment
I Couldnt figure out what So all I
Could do was Cry day in and day out
and Still never understood why. Because
of his wrong doing I had no trust in
men for a very long time because I
felt unworthy of love I felt as if
no-one Could or would love me
I was 16 no Job no education
and a baby with nothing when he
left me I felt as if I Couldn't go on
I thought I would die for sure
Cause I turned by back on every
one to please him so I had no
friends So not only did I feel lonely
I was lonely and it hurt Cause I
had no-one to talk to about the
heart Ache I was feeling it was
feeling that I Cant imagine feeling
again

[redacted]

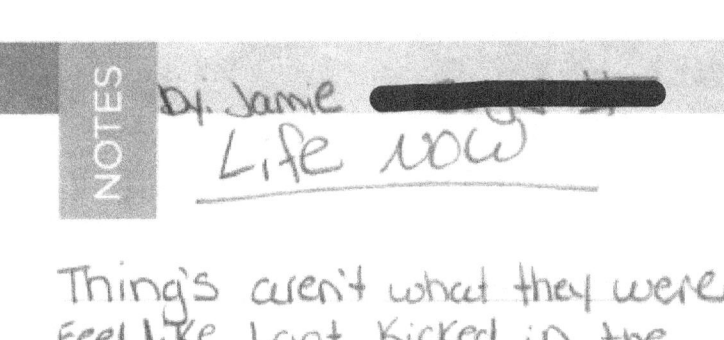

NOTES

Dr. Jamie [redacted]

Life now

Thing's aren't what they were
Feel like I got Kicked in the
ass with a spur
This path to gettin clean
is surely mother fucken mean
I'm doin all I possibly can
I almost grabbed my shit and ran
I feel empty in a lot of ways
But with these boys is
where my heart lays
All the people around me are in awe
Because they remember what they saw
I'm a different person now
I look in the mirror and I'm
straight up like, wow
my mind is in a different place
Still tryin to get use to this pace
Tryin to make our kid's proud
Screaming I'm fucking Sober
out loud!!

I've had many heartbreaks! One that stands out the most is when my ex took (our) child out of my life because of a fight we got into. The little girl wasn't mine biologically - but I loved her like she was. For a while I couldn't even think of her w/o breaking out in tears. I couldn't listen to certain songs or even speak her name (which is the same as mine - with "Lil" in the front of it. My ex was [illegible] still is very vindictive, extremely! Because I didn't want to be with and pursue her to reconciliate me and the child had to suffer for it. It was a sad time for me.

In all fairness I will admit - I was not a saint in this relationship.

I seriously can't stand my ex, however; because I still love that child I will always help the whore if she's in need.

Love is Amazing ☺

One of the first heartbreaks that I can recall is when I was in middle school. I was always a leader, confident and liked myself till seventh grade. Due to being around 25 pounds over weight, I was made fun of by my peers. I was called fat, ugly, a whale, and Shamoo amongst many other names. Kids were cruel and played jokes, games, and pranks, not only behind my back, but to my face. I felt anxious a lot due to this, so my social life became a huge trigger for anxiety. I still chose to feel accepted, cool, popular, & loved, so I did anything I had to do to keep them as friends & in the "clique" w/ them. The emotions I felt during & thru all of this can be described as: confused, defenseless, degraded, didnt measure up, embarressed, fear, humiliated, hurt, crushed, vulnerable, rejected, mistreated, lost, and insecure.

Luckily, by the grace & love of God, I do not let this effect me today & love myself. I have grown stronger, know my identity in Christ, and used this to make me into the amazing woman I am today. In sum, this is one of the first major "heartbreaks" I encountered in my life.

[redacted]

No

My first love I met when I was 12. I was with him until he got murdered I was 21, I've never recovered from this my life was spiraled out of control since. My heart still aches when I think of him.

[redacted]

My name Is Danni[redacted] I am a 34 year old female, Born In Gary, Indiana.

The very first time a piece of my heart was broken. I was 3 years old still living In Gary, Indiana. My family was at my Grandmas house I dont remember why. family dinner, or my Grandma was watching us? Not sure. Eit[h]er way My Grandma owned a little ranch style home, and In her house, she had a very big finished basement that had a room In the back that her adopted boys used as a bedroom.

One of those boys, took me Into that room. I vaguely remember him getting me to get In the bed with him. I remember him putting his penis In my face and telling me to suck on It. I remember It barly fitting In my mouth, how It was hard and I almost choked on It. I remember how he had my head under the covers as he lay on the bed. I also remember how someone walked In. Till this day I do not know who It was. If they new I was there a not. but they did what they had to do, said what they had to say and left. mean while he was pushing down on my head so hard that I could [illegible] breath. I felt like I was suffocating, I couldnt move, speak, scream, I couldnt [illegible]

Swallow. I after who ever It was left, he resumed action as If nothing ever happend.

I never new that what was happining was wrong. I dont even remember If that was the first time, last time, It It went on for years, If It lasted minutes or hours.

I do know that this man, boy at the time that did this, was someone that I trusted, My mom trusted, My Grandmother trusted.

I blocked It out for most of my life, I tried to live a normal life, but as I got older I started doing things that I new weren't right. I didn't even tell my mom untill last year in 2016. I held It in untill It destroyed me. It turned my life upside down.

Now I sit here, October 2017 an Inmate in the Kent County Correctional Facility, writing a piece of my life, That ended me up right where I am today.

I Can only think of how that damaged 3 year old little girl still lives Inside of me today. How I have ruined relationships, How I have never really loved myself. How I had completly had given up on life.

I will never forget that November day, it had been eight long months my little Isabella fighting for her life. She had a rare form of Leukemia and we spent most of those 8 months in Helen DeVos. It hurt me so much watching my daughter suffer so much and in that time I grew very angry with God and truly lost my faith. The pastor of our church visited everyday and I started to excuse myself I didn't want to hear what he had to say.

November 23, 2016 as I was holding Isabella she said "mommy don't hate God" an hour later at the age of 6 she passed away. Her last words to me has changed my life forever. During her pain and sorrow she was selfless wanting my relationship with God to be mended. I miss my daughter more than anything in this world. Her faith to the very end taught me a life long lesson; death here on earth isn't final when you have Jesus as your savior. I was reminded God has a plan for us. My relationship with God is stronger then ever and if I never had to face this storm I can't gaurentee my relationship with God would be the same but now I can cling to His promises I will see Isabella once again in Heaven.

[redacted]

[redacted]

My name is Haleigh [redacted], born May 11th, 1994. Last year I went through a struggle that forever changed me as a person and made me question my faith in God. April 27th, 2016 I found out I was pregnant. My baby dad and I were filled with happiness. 3 weeks later we went to the doctors and found out we were expecting twins. The happiest day of my life turned to the worst 9 months I have ever had. I got through my first trimester of my pregnancy and got kicked out of where I was staying because my baby daddy was sneaking into my bedroom and my roomates mother didn't like that. I was devastated. What was I going to do? How could I be so worthless I let myself lose my only place to stay. Let my baby dad tell it I was the most worthless piece of shit to walk the earth. How was I going to take care of my family? I was worthless. All I seen when I looked at myself was a worthless piece of shit. I hopped from hotel to hotel after this. Working my ass off to pay for my baby dad and I to have a place to stay. He would start picking fights with me after a while. He called me a whore, told me his kids weren't his (but they looked just like him), I was a slut, whore, liar, fat piece of shit, and worthless. The mental abuse turned into physical abuse. He would hit me, slam me against walls. My back teeth are missing because of him. I started to flinch when guys raised their hands next to me. 8 months pregnant I found out my baby dad had another women pregnant. Due 4 months after me. He had been fucking and talking to multiple women for a while and coming home to me at night telling me he loved me. The night I found out all the dirt he had done my heart broke in my chest, it felt like the wind had been knocked out of me, all my blood drained from my face as I fell to my knees. I couldn't breathe and tears were flowing from my eyes uncontrollably. The man I loved betrayed me. The man I did everything for and taken care of took my heart from my chest and crumbled it in his hands. Until I had no love left. I truly was worthless. I felt like I wasn't a women. I couldn't please, love, or take care of my man enough to make him love me, like I loved him. I didn't trust no man, I couldn't find myself loving anyone. His seeds I was carrying became a reminder of him everyday. I almost started to resent them. Not even giving him his 1st born sons could make him love me and stay. To be faithful to me. I couldn't trust anyone and he did that. I had no love for anyone or anything. He did that. I felt worthless, I felt like a piece of shit, I felt like dirt. He did that. I let him beat me and call me names because I thought that was one of his ways for him to show me he loved me. I couldn't be around a man who raised his voice or a hand without me flinching. He did that. I lost faith in myself as a women. He did that. Because of him I degraded myself. I cried myself to sleep everynight. Prayed to God to make the hurt go away. Asked him every night What did I do? For him to treat me how I did. How did I fail. Because of [redacted] I trust a little less. I can't love fully or love how people want me to love them. I used to cry myself to sleep holding my babies. Praying they didn't look at me the way their father did. Even though he made me suffer for, forever it felt like. He made me strong. God gave me my children. He gave me my wonderful fiance. God didn't promise happiness without pain. I never thought I could be happy again. Even though a little piece of my soul will still be missing. I will forever need to smoke my pain away, to be on anti-anxiety meds, I will always be cautious with my love and trust. All because a man didn't know how to be a MAN.

[redacted]

My name is ~~[illegible]~~ Kaya. This grandchild
has been through a lot in her
lifetime. I met my first husband when
I was only 15. He was [illegible] older
and I was too young & naive to
see what a person he was. Over time
he was able to get me to think I was
worthless, pretty, smart and I was whatever he
wanted me. He made sure I had no
friends and isolated me. All while I was
thinking I was just busy working 2 jobs
to support us and taking care of the kids.
The emotional and physical abuse was
tolerated until one day he decided to go
after my 11 year old daughter. When he
took her down and was beating her on
the ground I knew I had to get us out.
I packed her and [illegible] up and left right
away. We lived in a [illegible] room efficiency
apartment. My husband stalked us,
threatened us, tried every intimidation
method he could to get us back under
his control. I had a restraining order
on him during the divorce that he
constantly walked through. He changed
his game [illegible] to [illegible] me to
family, friends, [illegible] entire
community [illegible] in

[illegible] what he would say and recal to scene [illegible]. He had the [illegible] and older kids convinced I was a alcoholic even though I don't drink, and a adultress so I would get excommunicated from church. The one place he never went to until he found he could con wealthy people out of money at weekly bible study. I took care of my mom in my home for 25 years along with my kids. He decided to jump into bed with a selfish self centered sister who loves to lie & destroy people and made up a story that I wasn't spending mom's money on her. She used her position at the sheriff dept to get my [illegible] & arrested for elder abuse. Never ever encountering the law before I hired a attorney. I figured all would be ok, but the judge believed her vicious story in her statement and gave me a year in jail. I now have to rebuild my life as a felon, find a job, car, home but I will survive because I have God. With God anything is possible. He put me here for a reason. I'm sure I will be blessed when I get out and be able to show my ex & ex family that evil does not w[illegible]

As I got older, I started learning how to love with my heart and not my eyes. I grew up hearing every insult about black people and gay people. The racial and hate slurs came out of my dad's mouth. I remember it starting when I was about 15 years old. My favorite type of music was hip hop and rap. I loved Tupac and Lil wayne, I had a CD player in my room and listened to it often. My dad used to come in my room and tell me to turn down that nigger music. I was young and didn't know any better, so I just did what he asked me to do. He's my dad, he knows whats best for me is what I thought to myself. As I got older and started making new friends, I found myself hanging out with people that liked "nigger music" as my dad referred to rap. My dad would talk down on my black friends and tell me how they are bad people and in to drugs. Although he continued to say inappropriate comments about the things I liked and who I choose to become friends with. My dad made me feel like I was wrong about what I liked and said I was disrespecting him. I had tried to talk to my mom about my feelings because of how my dad was treating me. She had told me that my dad didn't like black people and that I should stay away from them because I'll piss him off. The only person I could turn to was my sisters and they never judged me because they were also

2

frowned upon by our dad. Not because of who they were with but because of the choices they made. In his eyes we weren't allowed to make mistakes and that being perfect was possible. It was possible if we did what he said. When I was 20 years old, I reconnected with this guy who used to sit next to me in 10th grade. He became very interested in me and pursued me until I became his girlfriend. My parents weren't happy for me, especially my Dad. As we started dating I became distant with my parents and started spending all of my free time with my boyfriend. Whenever I was gone from home my mom would send me texts asking when I'll be coming home or why I would be gone all day. My parents interfered with my relationship, they were not supportive. Whenever I was home my dad would make crazy remarks at the dinner table without being direct. He would say black people just cheat, abuse, and take money from women. He tried to say things in hope that I would change mind about my boyfriend but heart was already stuck on him. I fell in love with him and he always supported me and never made feel wrong about my feelings. My Dad broke my heart when he told me that if I wanted to continue dating him that I had to move out with him. It hurt that he didn't care about my happiness and that he was so quick to throw me out. When I had to tell my boyfriend

3.

the news they gave me. he told me I could live with him. My heart and mind were aching because I believed they would love me unconditionally like most parents did. I was only with my boyfriend for about 4 months. When I had moved out the next morning they didn't speak to me or wake up to say good bye. When I moved my things in to my boyfriends place, I laid in the bed and broke in to tears. I will never forget my first true heart break. I will teach my children to love with their hearts and not their eyes

(1)

Hello, my name is Kimberly [redacted] And I'm actually going to tell you about something that I never like to talk about, let alone to complete strangers. When I met the author of the book, you are reading now. She said she was writing a book about first heart breaks.

As I got to thinking, it wasn't my boyfriend, or someone I had a crush on & didn't like me back. It was my own flesh & blood. My dad, Bill Havener. You, You broke my heart. You started from the moment I could remember & never really stopped.

My first memory of you taking just a piece of my heart out is the day you finally made up my mom's mind to leave you. I was to young to be aware that you were cheating on her, & thats not what hurt. What hurt is when it was finally quiet & I came out of my room you were gone, & mom was in the shower with drops of blood every-where. Not your blood hers. That's where it began.

I remember not seeing you much,
& when it was time for my brother
and I to come to your house.
There was a women I knew
nothing about, along with four
other Kids in the house who
had the upper hand & me, my
brother ½ sister & other ½ brother
Who I will never claim. Were
left in the dark. 2nd time you
took another Piece of my heart,
we would come over & not
See you until Sunday mornings
because you & this new woman
were Partying the whole time. So
You weren't aware that the
half brother I won't claim
was molesting me. I got so used
to it, it was almost normal.
The next part of my heart I
didn't realize hurt so much was
When my mom got [redacted] and I
dressed up all nice & said it was your
Special day & you should be here
Soon. 3 hours went by & you
didn't show. I couldn't figure
out why mom took us out to
eat & rent movies so late like we
were getting a special treat.

The next weekend we came over (3)
& watched your wedding
on a video, & the women you
married, was the women you
were also cheating on my mother
with. All I could think was, why
wouldn't he want us there? Why
is it that Keith and I look
so dissapointed because everyone
around us was in this video,
laughing & having a good time
and him and I are just
there. Not because we were
wanted, because we had to be.
Throughout the years crumbs
were just falling like when you
bite into a cookie, but the
cookie was my heart. All of the
lies, saying you would show up
for our games but wouldn't &
"forgetting" to pick us up for your
weekends. And when we were
there, we litterally had to walk
on eggshells. I could tell so
many more stories. Being in
2nd grade telling me you were

going to hang my "pissy" bed
Sheets on the school flagpole for
everyone to see. Giving my step
sister cards when she felt down
& telling me to toughen up.

But these next two things
was my final straw for the
cookie to be in complete crumbs

Since I was 13, I have been
in & out of the hospital for
suicidal attempts. The first time I
was in there as inpatient
they did a drug test & found
methamphamine (crystal meth) in
my system. That brother who
molested me for 3 years also
introduced me to a new
escape method. Well
I finally let everything out thats when
my mom & stepdad had expected
Some form of sexual abuse with
my sexual past. Since they found out
I lost my virginity at 13*.

When I went to my dads house (5) when I was released from the hospital, he yelled at me. His exact words, "Do you want me to go to prison for the rest of my life?" Me, "...No..." Him, "Then Knock it off with the bullshit." Absolutley nothing about the meth nothing about anything. To make it all worse, he wouldn't contact me for about a month, after all of my useless attempts, he finally messaged me via FACEBOOK, I wasn't even worthy of a call. He asked me, "What do you want? You aren't my problem anymore!" And thats when I didn't have even close to a heart, it was broken, gone. I didn't know how to feel, all of my theories of him wanting nothing to do with me came true, except I was a problem, to be exact, I was a drunken bowling night mistake.

So although he broke me completely.
This book is also about how did
I overcome this heartbreak. I
overcame with realizing all the good
I had without him. When he isn't
here to bring me down, everything
around me brightens up. I came to
learn that my step father made
me realize what it was like to
have an actual loving father. I
am just as lucky to have that
as alot of children don't.
He may have broke me, but
damn he made me 10X stronger.
The final thing that I want to
make very clear, is sometimes it is
easier to let the one you love,
go. Because the pain you feel
when your consistently fighting for
them is constant. But the pain
you feel when you make the decision
to let them go, is only for a little
while. Thank you.

The major events in my life
that mark me so I could learn
how to appreciate and value life.
I was 14 when my life was
marked by one of the most
Valuable, person in my life and He
decide to rape me and tell me to
forget it like if never happen. My
mom never believe me and when
She found out our relationship broke.
At the age of 17 I had an
abortion that til this day I can't
forgive myself for it !!. But at
18 I met the LOVE of my life, I
(thaught). He was not handsome or
Cute or had a job but he had
Something that I LOVE and it was
that he was the leader of a gang.
So we date and even thou I didn't
like to many stuff that he was doing
It was to late for me to back out. At
age 21 had my son and even thou I
wanted to leave him and try but I
couldn't I was to scare. After going
thru so much with him and his gang.
Drive byes, fights, guns, Drugs, hoes and
having 3 kids by him I decide to
leave him when I caught him

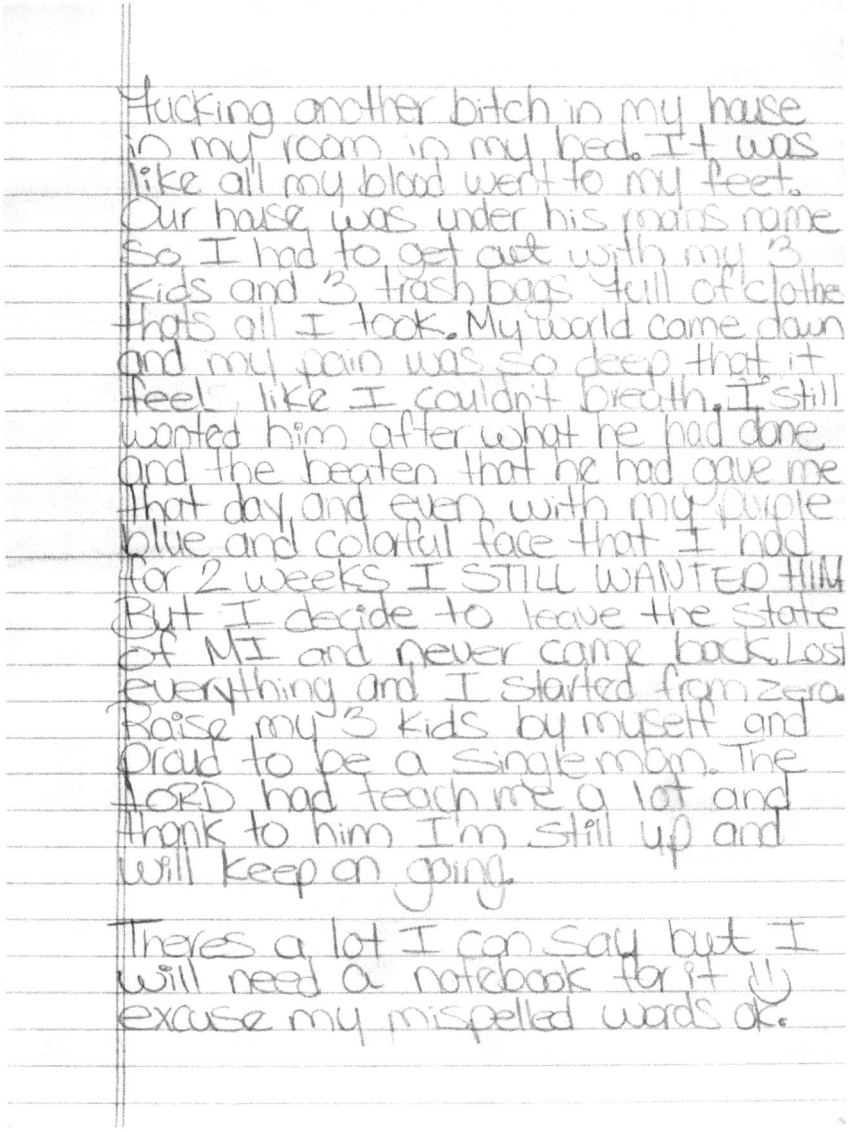

Fucking another bitch in my house in my room in my bed. It was like all my blood went to my feet. Our house was under his moms name so I had to get out with my 3 kids and 3 trash bags full of clothe thats all I took. My world came down and my pain was so deep that it feel like I couldn't breath. I still wanted him after what he had done and the beaten that he had gave me that day, and even with my purple blue and colorful face that I had for 2 weeks I STILL WANTED HIM But I decide to leave the state of MI and never came back. Lost everything and I started from zero. Raise my 3 kids by myself and proud to be a single mom. The LORD had teach me a lot and thank to him I'm still up and will keep on going.

Theres a lot I can say but I will need a notebook for it :) excuse my mispelled words ok.

I had a friend who was like my brother we grew up together he called my mom in 2012 he was on the run. he move to arizona with our mutual friend things didn't work out so he moved to detroit with his mom it [illegible] work there so he [illegible] to move with me [illegible] the [illegible] everything with mom so I asked her she said yes he came to grand rapids [illegible] to my house we caught up cause it been a couple months since we seen each other I was so happy he was [illegible] with me he [illegible] and call a few girls cause he wanted to chill with some females [illegible] up to [illegible] cause I was [illegible] so I couldn't go he called a girl they said they [illegible] we played 2K and took a couple shots till his ride pulled up. before he left he told me he loved me and don't fall asleep cause he was coming back. So I stayed up at night on the phone [illegible] almost [illegible] I fell asleep, woke up to a [illegible] phone call saying my brother was found dead on a back porch [illegible] [illegible] I [illegible] [illegible] [illegible] [illegible] my self [illegible] [illegible]

My heart messed up and I got trust issues because of my boy death I'll never trust a soul

My first love!

I was young and very permiscuous. Because I was so permiscuous two brothers thought it would be A good idea to show me How to get money for sexual acts. So I stood on A street corner for about 25 minutes. I really wasn't sure what to do or what to say. I did know I didn't want to go far. I wanted to stay in eye contact of the two brothers. So the guy just parked at the end of the street. I was with him about 5 minutes and made 60$. I gave each brother 20$ And told them thank you and to go on their way and they did. I started running away from home and found myself sleeping in a crack house and standing on the street corner for hours on out for chump change. At this crack house I met A man. He was a crack dealer. It was love at first sight I thought. He would take me with him periodically. this would really make Me Happy. I was always so full of Joy when I was with him. His joy was money I got to realize that real fast. So I eventually would go stand on the street corner more often to get money to be with him More often. When in all reality he really wasn't spending any More or any less time with me. Then the truth was finally came out. He was in love with someone already. He even had a kid on the way. I was literly 14 years old at the time and I was broken.

(1)

IM TAMMY G. I GREW UP IN A DISFUNCTIONAL FAMILY, MOM & DAD WERE DIVORCED SINCE I WAS 3. MOM HAD ALOT OF DIFFERENT MEN. I WAS EXPOSE TO ABUSE, EMOTIONALY, SEXUALY, AND PHYSICALY. I SAW MY DAD ON VISITATIONS IN MY CHILDHOOD, HE WAS GOOD TO ME. HE WAS A HIPPIE, HE HAD LONG HAIR. HE SMOKED WEED AND SOLD IT. I WAS AROUND ROOMS AND CARS SO FULL OF SMOKE I COULD NOT SEE. I GREW UP AN ADDICT AND ALWAYS HAD LOTS OF BOYFRIENDS SOMETIME I WAS NOT ONLY A 2 TIMER, I WAS A 10 TIMER. I WAS MARRIED ONCE. ALL MY MEN WERE ADDICTS. I STARTED OUT AT 13 WITH WEED AT 16 I MOVED IN WITH A MAN WHO WAS 29, HE SOLD WEED. WE MUST HAVE SMOKED 10 JOINTS A DAY. I WAS WITH HIM FOR 9 YEARS. HIS NAME WAS DICK MOORE, WE FOUGHT ALOT. HE PUSHED ME AROUND, HELD ME DOWN, CHASED ME, TACKLED ME. NEVER HIT ME. OUR LAST FIGHT I THREW A GLASS PLATTER ON THE FLOOR, AND HE PICKED UP A SHARP PIECE OF THE PLATTER AND THREATENED ME WITH IT. HE ALSO WAS GOOD AT FLIPPING THE BED UPSIDE DOWN WHILE IM IN IT IGNORING HIM. WHEN HE LEFT TO GO TO WORK I WAS CRYING. I FELT UNLOVED UNWANTED, I WAS ANGRY I WANTED TO →

(2)

LEAVE HIM. WE HAD 1 CHILD TOGETHER, DIXON WAS THEN 3 YRS OLD. I CALLED A SHELTER - EVERY WOMAS PLACE IN MUSKEGON. I WAS CRYING TELLING THEM OF OUR FIGHT. THEY TOLD ME TO COME STAY AT THE SHELTER AND THAT THEY COULD HELP ME GET FOOD AND RENT ASSISTANCE FOR MY OWN APARTMENT, AND THAT IS WHAT I DID. I HAD A POLICE OFFICER TAKE ME TO MEET A LADY FROM THE SHELTER (AT McDONALDS

AFTER HAVING MY OWN APARTMENT I WAS LONELY. I STARED OUT THE WINDOW WISHING DICK MY SONS FATHER WOULD COME TO SEE US. BUT HE DIDNT. I WAS SAD & DEPRESSED OF THE 9 YEARS I WAS WITH HIM, HE HAD STRONG CONTROL OVER ME. I NEVER HAD A JOB. NEVER SAW MY FAMILY. I WAS MAD AT MY MOM FOR HOW I WAS RAISED. WHEN DIXON WAS 4 MY MOM CALLED ME TO PATCH UP WHAT HAPPENED. WE HAD A NICE BIRTHDAY PARTY FOR DIXON. SHE WAS A BETTER GRAMA THEN A MOM.

my name is Dana [redacted]
I was born November 6 1976
The first time I ever had felt an
emotional pain I couldn't get
over was when I met a guy
named Matt. We met Aug 2006
everything was amazing in the beginning
just as I wanted it to be and
pictured a perfect life with him
until later on in our relationship
I found out that he was an
alcholic a very bad one and
then everything had falling apart
He had became verbal and physical
towards me emotionally abusive. In
those situations it made me feel
weak, terrible, worthless, downgraded. Matt called me a whore
because I had 2 kids with 2 different
men and I looked in the mirror
and ask myself am I a whore...
after that I cried my eyes out
for days my eyes where puffy
and swollen. I never had anyone
ever talk that way to me before

from that situation I lost self
worth it took me a long time to
build the women I am today.
I think if matt could have
stayed sober our relationship
would of been benifical to both
of us. I feel that in that
time of my life was a turning
point if he wasn't emotionlly
abusive I wouldn't be ok with
disrespecting my children's father's
and emotionally abusing them treating
my kid's father's like shit I feel
that karma came back to me

[redacted]

Sorry

The choices we make
the laws that we break
the hurt that I caused
for going A-wall:
I truly am Sorry...
Trying to hold it together,
knowing this stay isn't 4 ever
I wanna hug my kids
and just 4 get what I did:
I truly am Sorry...
Everything happens for a reason
in 2 months I'll be leaving,
leaving this life way behind me,
for I am a woman who is free:
I truly am Sorry...
I'm changing my life around
never wearing a frown,
God is good and helped me thru this
but I never will forget what I did:
I truly am Sorry...
I'm ending this with a goodbye + godbless
When I get out, that will be the test,
to make choices that are right
with the ALMIGHTY GOD by my SIDE:
*THANK YOU JESUS...

2/12/1
Pm

09/30/2017

"Wishing you the best"

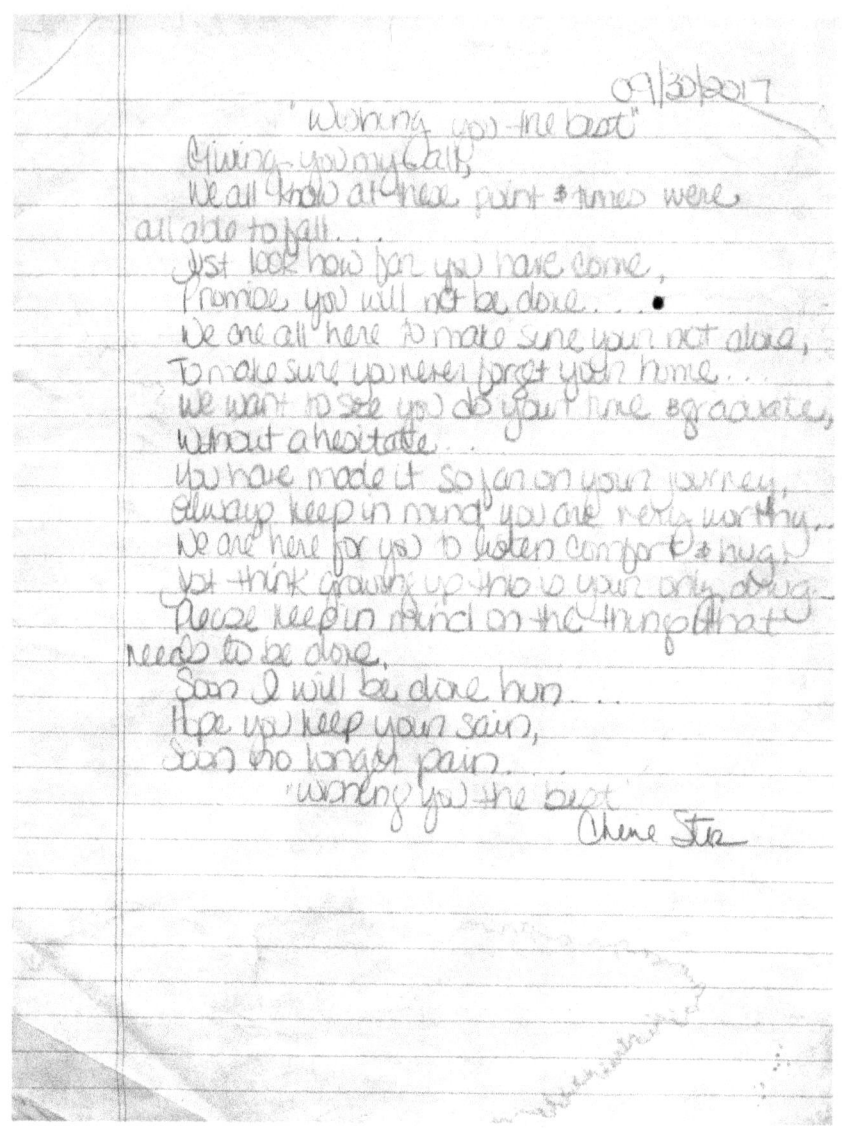

Giving you my all,
We all know at these point & times were
all able to fall...
Just look how far you have come,
Promise you will not be done...
We are all here to make sure your not alone,
To make sure you never forget your home...
We want to see you do your time & graduate,
without a hesitate...
You have made it so far on your journey,
always keep in mind you are very worthy...
We are here for you to listen comfort & hugs,
you think growing up this is your only drug...
Please keep in mind on the things that
needs to be done.
Soon I will be done hun...
Hope you keep your sain,
Soon no longer pain.
"wishing you the best
Cherie Star

Jan 17

Let see where do I Start... It Seems to me that this life of mine has been full of heart break. From growing up with a mom with Hepatitis C, Which back then was a terminal illness. And having to Visit her in a hospital bed. Scared that everytime I left the hospital' that it was going to be the last time I would see her. Then having to go to school and put a smile on my face like nothing was wrong. That's why I never miss the chance to tell the People I care about that I love them. Because I know that life is a fragile thing and nothing last forever.

I Remember I was acting a fool when I was like 12-13. I Just got out of Juvenile an She sat me down and Read her letters to me that she wrote for me and my bro when the Doctors told her she was going to die. That was one of the hardest things to hear still to this day. What do you do with that sh!t? I was actually mad at her for doing that. I never thought about it til now but her being here still is a miracle.

Another heart breaking situation, Was finding my bro Sid dead. That was my right hand man. I would of taken a bullet for him. I actually took a drug charge for him. He taught me alot, Some good and Some bad.

(1)

We've been to war together. When he got paralyzed everyone left all his friends his girls. I didn't tho that shit made us closer. I use to take him with me everywhere, It was almost like the Roles where reversed, I was the Big Bro now. We'd go out I use to make the hoes dance on him at the strip club. he use to love that shit, we'd have so much fun that was my big bro... But everytime we would get back to the crib, and I would pick him up out of his chair to put him in his bed. He would always tell me he was sorry, as if he was a burden to me or something. That would fuck me up because we was just having fun I guess Reality would kick in that he was paralyzed from the neck down. He would tell me he wanted to die, I'd tell him stop playing, but I could see in his eyes he was serious and he had gave up. I sat and watch him die a lil bit everyday. Then one day I went in to get him out of bed to start his day. I stood by his bed and seen he wasn't breathing. I looked at his face he was gone he was so cold. I know he had to of been dead for hours. I knew there was nothing that could be done. Me and my sis Jen tryed CPR. The medics came and said the same thing there's nothing left.

(2)

After every one left we was waiting for the People to come get his body. I sat in the room with him alone and talked to him for about a hour. I said I bet your Punk Ass is up there dancing right now and I'm down here all sad and shit.
I waited until the People got there Put my hand on the top of his head told him I loved him and I'd miss him and that was that.
[illegible]
Then my Pops Killed himself that was Rough. That happen not even six months after my bro died. It hurt worst the fact that he did it to himself. I remember the day it happen. I talked to him earlier. I asked what he was up to? He told me Joe I'm Just tired. My dad was addicted to Pills and he didn't have any. I was selling Pills at this time in my life. He asked if I had any I lied and said I didn't. I wanted him to get off of them. I still think if I would have Just gave him some he would still be here I don't Know.
Any'ways I was beefing with my Bm at the time, So I was staying at my Grandmother's Crib She was in AZ at the time So her house was empty.

3

I get a call from my Mom she was crying.
I asked her what was wrong? She said
Your dad is dead. I told her that cant be
I just talked to him. So I hung up called
my StepMother I asked her what happen?
She said she went down stairs and she found
him down there, she said the barrel of the
shot gun was still in his mouth and
the top of his head was gone. That Put me
in a real bad place and I didn't get better
until I meet my wife. Another Heart breaking
situation. Was coming to Prison. Getting all this
time and watching everybody change up on me...
It's heart breaking to sit in here and watch
everyone move on. Not that they shouldn't Becuase
it no ones fault but my own for being in here.
but you can't help to think that, thats suppose
be my life that someone else is living with my
wife. Or thats suppose to be my children. Heartbreak
is when you have 5 kids you consider to be
your kin and you only get to see 1 of them. Or
when you 150 miles away, but you might as well
be on the other side of the world beause aint
no one coming. Heart break is when you
love someone so much that when you see her
cry you cry.

(4)

Heart break is when you Know what would've been,
but this Prison shit made it so it can't be
anymore. Heart break is when your grasping on to
the last few threads of your Perfect life you had
before this Prison shit happened, because
you are scared of the heart break of loseing
the love of your life. Heart break is haveing
to let go of the person that made
you the happiest. Yea I Know alot
about heart Break

5

www.ingramcontent.com/pod-product-compliance
Lightning Source LLC
Chambersburg PA
CBHW051343020726
47501CB00007B/2247
9780578886992